Why Gather?

D1496141

Dr. Kenneth Kuhn
405-255 Wellington Cres
Winnipeg, MB R3M 3V4

Why Gather?

The Hope and Promise of the Church

Martha Tatarnic

CHURCH
PUBLISHING
INCORPORATED

Copyright © 2022 by Martha Tatarnic

All rights reserved. No part of this book may be reproduced, stored in a retrieval system, or transmitted in any form or by any means, electronic or mechanical, including photocopying, recording, or otherwise, without the written permission of the publisher.

Unless otherwise noted, the Scripture quotations are from New Revised Standard Version Bible, copyright © 1989 National Council of the Churches of Christ in the United States of America. Used by permission. All rights reserved worldwide.

Church Publishing
19 East 34th Street
New York, NY 10016

Cover design by Paul Soupiset, Soupiset Design
Typeset by Denise Hoff

Library of Congress Cataloging-in-Publication Data

Names: Tatarnic, Martha, author.
Title: Why gather? : the hope and promise of the church / Martha Tatarnic.
Description: New York, NY : Church Publishing, [2022]
Identifiers: LCCN 2022001333 (print) | LCCN 2022001334 (ebook) | ISBN 9781640655515 (paperback) | ISBN 9781640655522 (ebook)
Subjects: LCSH: Church. | Public worship. | Fellowship--Religious aspects--Christianity.
Classification: LCC BV600.3 .T38 2022 (print) | LCC BV600.3 (ebook) | DDC
    262--dc23/eng/20220210
LC record available at https://lccn.loc.gov/2022001333
LC ebook record available at https://lccn.loc.gov/2022001334

For Gordon & Cecilia,
Whose inquiring and discerning hearts
inspired this book.

Contents

Introduction

This book's initial spark came from bedtime conversations with my son Gordon, who was ten years old at the time and was struggling with his faith. I responded to his struggle, first by telling him his questions were good and faithful; at baptism, we pray that each newly minted Christian will grow to have an "inquiring and discerning heart." I said the prayer was being answered in his seeking and searching. He needed to know what we all need to know: there is blessing and love in both our belief and unbelief.

The second thing I said came right from my gut—it was instinct and nothing else. I advised him to stay close to the church. I am a priest of the Anglican Church of Canada, and as this book will show, I wear no rose-colored glasses when it comes to the church. I have despaired about it, I have wanted to leave it, I have been hurt by it. But in that moment, I knew a basic, burning truth: when I consider my own faith—why I believe in God and follow Jesus—it is because of the community of faith. Every tenet of our belief system is real and meaningful to me, not because of philosophical arguments or brilliant apologetics, but because of experience—because of how I see real flesh-and-blood people embody and bear witness to the things we believe.

That unalterable truth became a touchstone almost a year later when COVID-19 shut down the world, and I found myself embroiled in questions of whether I had a future in the church and whether that church had any sort of future ahead for itself. It became clear to me that my advice to Gordon was a reality check for me too. I couldn't leave the church, even if I wanted to. The church isn't the institution or the buildings, it's the living, breathing reality of the God Who Draws Near and is even now at work in the hot mess of our lives. As COVID-19 made clear, we are radically affected and infected by one another's oxygen and water vapors and germs and skin molecules, and at the same time our souls actually can't know and love God without one another.

But knowing that I need the church and can't really be whole in my relationship with God without it is not the same as choosing the church. It's not the same as embracing that hot mess with a sense of joy.

I wrote this book because of the church and for the church. This is my embrace of the reality of who we are, how God has been at work in us, why that matters, and how it might all be connected to an offering of joy and love—not just for ourselves but for the world. It is a clear-eyed, unsentimental love letter to the church I can't get away from, and that I can choose with joy once again.

In this love letter, I hope you find space to consider your own worries for the future of the church: the strain that puts on our leaders and congregations, the burn-out that is a constant risk in our clergy, the truths that COVID-19 revealed, and the change that we fight for in the institution. This book is going to name those realities but not dwell in them, because the truth of the church—of who we are and what we have to offer—isn't located in our institutional worries but in relationship with God, revealed in one another. And so my greater hope for you, the reader, is that the stories that form the core of this book, of God at work in real flesh-and-blood lives, will sharpen your own senses in their awareness of God's presence and activity. I hope these stories will be empowering to the people of our church in naming and claiming what this is really about: the God of love promising to walk with us, even now, in the fragile and uncertain circumstances of our lives.

That hope is a compass for the church going forward. The problems in the world are myriad and urgent. The future of the church has seemed, for several generations now, to be on shaky ground. Anxiety around decline can be a distressing and all-consuming reality, and it can be especially paralyzing when coupled with the distress and anxiety of the world in which we live. And yet, the reality of God's love and presence in the church and in our lives is unshakeable, is not in decline, and always and forever reminds us who we really are.

The reality of all of our lives, whether we like it or not, is that the world is set up for us to be biologically, spiritually, and emotionally affected by one another—even infected by one another. Whether we see it or not, God is already at work in our massive inextricably infected reality of what it is to be alive in this particular universe. Our lives are bound to one another, and God meets us right in the thick of that binding—in the joy and pain, the heartbreak and wonder and disappointment—of how we love and serve and mess up and try to live and eventually die.

That reality is the church's reality too. Not the church that could be or that we wish we were. The church that is. Let's start here; let's gather here. Let's lift up and tune in and look again for the God who is drawing near in the mess, the infection, the binding, the truth of how we are stuck together, and the truth of how we can choose one another. This is what matters; this is what can't be taken away. This is what must be centered in the life of the church if we are to go forward into all of the uncertainty of the future with a hope that doesn't just bless us, but also blesses our world.

I

Everything Is
on the Table

CHAPTER 1

Stuck

March 6, 2020

I was out running on March 6, 2020, when Cheryl called.

I was a few miles in, which is important to note, because the thing I always say about running is that the first ten minutes are the worst. In those first ten minutes, I am a prisoner in my own mind. No matter how physically fit, no matter how much I know in my head that I enjoy running, when I first put shoe to pavement, my lungs feel like they are going to explode, my muscles ache and rebel, I am sure I have to pee even though I went just before leaving the house, and all of the miles that I have planned stretch endlessly and impossibly in front of me. If I can stick it out for those first ten minutes, what feels like prison opens into a surprising freedom.

Getting to that freedom takes a major shift in perspective. Every single time I go out, I need to know that my mind is going to take me down every available rabbit hole about why I shouldn't be there, why I can't do it, what isn't working about the conditions in front of me, why this whole enterprise is doomed from the start. Yet somehow what happens after those rabbit holes feels like nothing short of a miracle. It's not that I go somewhere different, it's that I land somewhere real. My body gets into enough of a rhythm that my mind lets go of "what if" and "why am I here anyway." What is actually happening takes over from the mind game of wondering what else I could be doing or what might lie around the corner.

I was nicely into that rhythm on March 6. My plan was to run and then come home and pack, but at that moment I was lost in the mix of shoe on pavement. My "Under Pressure" ringtone interrupted me midstride. When I saw Cheryl's name on the display, my mood and mind frame shifted abruptly. I knew the news wasn't good. I could hear the hesitation and worry in her voice. She had tried to engage me a number of times over the previous weeks, and I had refused to listen.

"Martha, we really need to talk."

In two days, Cheryl and I were supposed to get on a plane to fly to Jerusalem for a ten-day pilgrimage to the Holy Land. COVID-19 had been simmering in the daily news cycle for months. "It's a nothing burger," I had quipped to friends and acquaintances, thinking myself clever for not getting caught up in the hype and fearmongering. Many news stories predicting dire illnesses, deadly insects, and various other upheavals have cycled through our collective consciousness and have left us relatively unscathed. I assumed the relentless worry about this virus was going to go much the same way.

But that wasn't why I was insisting that we fly to Jerusalem. It wasn't even that I was so totally invested in the opportunity to walk among the same places as Jesus and to see with my own eyes scenes from the Bible stories I had been reading my whole life come into three-dimensional color. I understood, as Cheryl had been trying to tell me, that we could reschedule.

The truth was that I was desperate to get away. I wanted to unplug. I wanted to be immersed in a different world. I wanted to physically and literally leave everything behind and be given permission to be away from my life. I had been running myself ragged. I had published and promoted a book; I had helped lead a massive initiative at our church to open a resource center for the troubled young people in our downtown; I was a full-time working mom in charge of a busy urban parish.

Even that wasn't really the problem, however. There is a time of life for these pedal-to-the-metal lifestyles; there is a season for that constant state of juggling around which parts of our overflowing plates get the lion's share of our attention at any given time. The problem was that I didn't feel like any of it was working anymore.

I'm good at organization and strategically putting ideas into action. But I am even better at following my gut. I govern the biggest decisions of my life by instinct. I can feel the power of an idea as a burning energy in the pit of my stomach, making my whole body tingle. When I get that feeling, I know I need to act.

For the last few months, that gut instinct had been failing me. My entire job had devolved into one never-ending task of conflict management as my supposedly good ideas were causing nothing but misunderstanding and anger. I needed to get on that plane. I needed a break. I needed it now. I knew what Cheryl was going to say. I stopped running. A crushing weight of disappointment settled on my chest before she even had to say the words.

"We can't go," she said. "It's not safe."

"Is It Because of That Coronavirus Thing?"

I understood I would be stuck at home, but I didn't understand much else. I was shocked when, later that day, the schools announced, just before our kids came home for spring break, that they would remain on break for two weeks beyond their scheduled time off. I wildly tried to fill up my suddenly empty week with overnights in Toronto and fun plans for Cheryl's birthday, which we were supposed to have celebrated in the Holy Land.

Others were slow to understand too. My Mom and I discussed the school closures: "Maybe if everybody just stays home for a few weeks, then we can put this behind us," we commented naively. We had a packed party at the church that night, a farewell reception for Michael, a friend and colleague at the church leaving for another position. We had no idea that this would be the last such gathering for the foreseeable future. We breathed each other's air and smudged our germs all over plates, glasses, and smooth surfaces with abandon. When I shared the news with a few people at the party asking about my canceled trip, they expressed mild surprise that we weren't going.

"Is it because of that coronavirus thing?" they asked.

From that evening onward, plans fell through one by one, and the world began the domino effect of shutdown. Even trips to Toronto became unsafe. Restaurants, shopping centers, theaters, public spaces of all kinds, became spookily empty. By the following weekend, just eight days later, we received the dictum to close our churches to in-person worship.

There was much hand-wringing about this most of all, but we comforted ourselves with happy thoughts about how good it would be when we could be together again and have a big party after the service to celebrate getting through a tough patch. Duchesses Kate and Meghan were pictured gloveless and shaking hands with their adoring public after a royal event around this time, and they were framed as brave and compassionate—like Diana before them, hugging AIDS patients—because the threat of illness wasn't standing in the way of their willingness to be close to their people.

"I feel so guilty," people said to me over the phone and by email, which became the only ways we had to connect. Our church is full of people who devote their lives to service, to their care for others, to being in the thick of the community's need.

"People are dying. Frontline workers are risking their lives. And I'm just stuck at home."

Our church's daily breakfast program had to move to a takeout model, closing the in-person dining that was so much a feature of the compassion we were seeking to offer people—not just food, but a warm and safe place to sit and to be fed.

"We're acting on fear," was the lament. "We're not acting out of love for God's people."

As the first few days of shutdown turned into the first few weeks of the global pandemic, our collective understanding shifted. Masks, physical distance, closed doors, and stay-at-home orders all became not just regular features of our lives, but also the new signs of how we cared. Slowly, we started to realize our changed state of affairs was not going to be over in a few weeks or even a few months.

Is This a Prison or a Path to Freedom?

"Do you actually enjoy running, Mommy?" my daughter, Cecilia, has asked on more than one occasion, wrinkling their nose in disbelief. Although I talk a lot about how much I love running, I understand their skepticism. At their age, I also would have been horrified by the thought of doing this for any reason other than being forced to in gym class. But the thing that I have come to love about running is the same thing that I have loved about being a musician, and it's the same thing that I recognize as being essential to the spiritual life as well. When you're practicing scales or kneeling in prayer or engaging in any sort of discipline that requires a lot of showing up and going through the motions, there is the opportunity to get so hemmed in by the specific boundaries of what that discipline requires that a new sort of freedom opens up. Instant gratification is easy to come by, but a lot of what makes life worth living requires a measure of patience and openness to stick it out past beginnings that aren't comfortable or fun.

This is at the heart of the spiritual tradition of the wilderness. What looks like the wild and wandering circumstances that never would have been our choosing is actually terrain that is ripe for finding out who we really are. Jesus threw himself into the rigorous discipline of a forty-day wilderness period after his baptism and prior to beginning his public ministry. I wonder if he knew, though, that this wilderness was leading somewhere. I wonder if he felt like he chose the wilderness or if it found him.

More than that, I wonder what sort of wilderness he experienced prior to that forty-day fast. He was thirty years old, we understand, when he began his public ministry. This man who had so much ballyhoo about him when he was born was, by first-century standards, practically an old man by the time anything began to happen for him. Did he feel stuck? Did he wonder what he was doing or where he was going? Did he wish that something would happen? Did he fear that this something might not be what he wanted? In those thirty years leading up to when it all got started, did he know that being stuck was also part of it? That he had to have those quiet, unremarkable years in order to be clear enough about who he was that he could offer himself for the world?

I might willingly go out and subject myself to the relentless pavement pounding, to the boredom, to the numbing repetition of long-distance running, and I might know that this is going to allow me—body, mind, and spirit—to become centered in ways that are refreshing and transformative and freeing. That doesn't mean that I don't often wonder what I'm doing out there or wish I were somewhere else. It also doesn't mean that when I have felt stuck, bored, anxious, depleted, and frantic about other circumstances in my life, circumstances not of my choosing, that I have been able to keep track in those times that something good and necessary might actually be unfolding too.

I happened to feel stuck at the same time that most of the world was literally stuck. Most of us had our experiences of panic to sort through as our minds went down the rabbit holes of doubt and distress in which we can so easily dwell when it looks like miles of unchosen terrain are stretching out relentlessly in front of us. The pain and suffering, the loss and fear of COVID was real and significant. It claimed millions of lives and livelihoods and it has left permanent marks on our souls. The cost of lockdown isolation on us spiritually and mentally is a cost that we will be grappling with for years to come. These are stark and difficult truths and not to be minimized.

Also, there was a potential gift in the sudden enforced discipline of having nowhere to go than to be exactly where we were. In churchier (or more Hollywood) language, we talk about apocalypse. Apocalypse isn't actually that fancy of a concept, even if it is a big word. It means a revealing. It is the pulling back of the curtain to unveil what has been true and real all along. Christians would begin talking about apocalypse a lot in the 2020 pandemic. We were inspired in part by the pictures from around the world of those busiest of public spaces suddenly looking like postapocalyptic ghost towns. But our faith also gave us language for accessing the spiritual invitation that might be on offer too. When you can't go anywhere, you can figure out who you really are. Hard truths were being revealed to us at a staggering rate: truths about who and what really matter, who and what hasn't mattered enough, who and what we want to matter more going forward.

Running gave me a new metaphor: ultrarealism, which is a technique long-distance runners use for mental fitness. It is the practice of seeing, accepting, and embracing the actual circumstances in which you find yourself.[1] It is about responding to the moment in front of you rather than the moment you worry might be coming or which circumstances you wished were different. When people talk about positive thinking, I instantly lose interest. Ultrarealism, however, isn't about training the mind to squeeze reality through the frames of any sort of rose-colored glasses. It's about getting real.

At the beginning of March 2020, it had been a few years since I had trained for any longer distance running races, and I had never heard of ultrarealism. I ended up clocking a lot of miles that year. Ultrarealism became important to me as a runner, but it became even more important to me in the wilderness in front of me as a priest and in front of us as a church. There were some things ahead for me to better understand. There was a pile of acceptance that had to be hard-earned. Figuring out any sort of embrace, joy, choice was still countless miles away. I didn't know it, but the church I wanted to fly away from was going to be key in my understanding of what was actually most real—not just for me, but for all of us.

Nowhere to Go

When Cheryl called on March 6, I was hell-bent on getting on that plane to Jerusalem because it felt like my life was coming apart at the seams. I didn't want to admit to anyone, least of all myself, why leaving it behind felt like the only solution. Instead, I had to stay put and figure some things out. I began considering that key components of my life might be up for negotiation. It

---

1   Matt Fitzgerald coins the term *ultrarealism* in his book, *The Comeback Quotient* (Boulder, CO: VeloPress, 2020), as a mental fitness technique that he applies particularly to endurance sports. I adapt his definition slightly in applying it to the life of the church.

was like I was at the bargaining table of life, with myself—and maybe God—the only one sitting across from me. I was putting stuff on that table that hadn't felt up for grabs for a long time.

The last time I had considered running from my calling to be a priest had been in the final months of seminary, with parish ministry and ordination right around the corner. My temptation then had been to stay in the academic world, where at least I had a whisper of a clue of what I was doing. A number of friends and professors encouraged me to join them in the writing, research, and teaching sphere.

I would have liked such a clear alternative at this juncture. With nowhere to go, no plane to catch, no getaway car, I was stuck. And in being stuck, I considered whether God was still calling me to be a priest or whether there might be something else I could do with my life. The burnout that had been creeping ever closer to my heart and soul didn't get any better with COVID. The question of whether I still had a way forward in leadership in the church was my constant companion—not just when our trip got canceled but for all of the coming year.

On March 8, Cheryl and I were supposed to fly to Jerusalem. We went to an overnight spa instead, comforting ourselves with a little treat while I nursed my crushing disappointment. We were sharing a glass of wine by the fireplace when my sister-in-law, Jessica, sent a text to ask where I was and if I was okay. She had heard the news that Jerusalem had just made the decision to shuttle every arriving visitor into a mandatory two-week quarantine. Were we safe at home, or had we gotten stuck?

Cheryl and I both shed a few tears and called loved ones to tell them of our near miss. As the snowball effect of COVID spread continued, we realized just how much of a near miss it really was. Well before that two-week quarantine would have expired, most international travel had ground to a halt. We heard stories of Canadians all over the world stuck abroad and massive government-led initiatives to extricate them from those situations and bring them home.

I had thought I was stuck staying home, but my perspective suddenly tilted to reveal just how stuck I might have become if I had gone away.

DISCUSSION QUESTIONS

1. Where were you and what were you doing when the COVID-19 pandemic became real to you? Can you look back on that time now amazed at how little you and we understood about what was happening?

2. "Instant gratification is easy to come by, but a lot of what really makes life worth living requires a measure of patience and openness to stick it out past beginnings that aren't comfortable or fun." Where do you experience the truth of this statement?

3. In our religious tradition, the wilderness is seen as ripe terrain for spiritual growth, for learning more about who we are and where our lives have gotten off track. Without minimizing the loss and horror of COVID, what do you think the pandemic taught us about who we are and how we have gotten off track?

4. Looking back on your life, are there times when you have felt stuck that have actually been important times of learning and growth for you?

5. Ultrarealism asks us to shift our focus from what you wish were different, or what you're worried might happen, to instead "see, accept, and embrace" the circumstances in which you actually find yourself. Martha gets this term from long-distance running, but how might this shift in focus be applicable to other aspects of life?

CHAPTER 2

A Bad Body Image

Religious Freedom

I grew up with piles of beautiful religious freedom. I wasn't forced to believe, either from my parents or from the pulpit. It was never suggested to me that if I didn't toe the line, I'd end up in hell. Faith was not presented as a threat, but an invitation. Dancing, boyfriends, nail polish, short skirts and low-cut tops, friends of all different backgrounds—there was room for all of it in the life of a Christian. I was allowed to read books and magazines that described very different lifestyles to that of my middle-class rural upbringing. I listened to every kind of music, even if it was slapped with the "Warning to Parents" label. I saw women in leadership and was encouraged to be a leader with a strong voice too. I understood that Jesus had female disciples and that encouraging women to be leaders was consistent with following Jesus. I read the Bible and saw that Jesus was a feminist. It was because of my Christian faith that in my grade 11 law class I argued for the rights of same-sex couples to adopt children, over and against most of my classmates who couldn't conceive of such a thing being possible or right, given that we lived in a small town where there wasn't any evidence of any out gay people.

This isn't the usual religious perspective that we hear. I didn't have to rebel against the things I had been taught. I also didn't have to find my way to the faith. I have had a lifelong relationship with God and connection to the church. That relationship hasn't been without its challenges and pain, but it was never forced on me. The belief to which I was invited had all kinds of room for me, for the whole me, and for my whole experience of what it is to be alive in this crazy world.

This beautiful religious freedom was a gift, and I am deeply grateful for it. I went through my own conversion at the age of fifteen, where suddenly the faith that I had been immersed in my whole life became of critical importance for me. The best way I can describe what happened is that I fell in love with Jesus. It was a relationship of mysterious and exhilarating love that compelled me not just to stay in the church, not just to imagine how the Christian faith might be the organizing principle of my life, but also to allow that faith to overturn my own hopes and dreams for my future and to say a (begrudging) "yes" to this nagging feeling that I was to be a priest.

Over the years, I have had to regularly convert to the Christian faith. Very few of us experience our faith as a won-and-done kind of thing. We have to keep rediscovering the truth of what we believe and decide whether we continue to stay committed.

Where I haven't had a lot of experience, and this is likely a cost of that beautiful religious freedom, is any sort of articulation of how believing might be of urgent importance. Urgency and fear are too often bound up in one another. Leaders in our tradition don't threaten people into believing. Hellfire and brimstone talk in our churches is rare. This has also meant there is very little talk of why faith might matter, beyond just a personal choice.

Decline and Distorted Thinking

I was looking for a good reason to stay in the church and in ministry when the pandemic hit. But the church was having her own struggles with articulating why any of this might matter. My questions about my life and my vocation, and my unhappiness in who I was and where I had found myself, were even more closely paralleled, if not inextricably linked, to the core questions that have been in front of us as the Church now for decades.

At the beginning of 2020, the future of the Church was looking shaky and some denominations were naming it explicitly. Those who get *The Anglican Journal*, our national Canadian church newspaper, received in their mailboxes just before Christmas 2019 an issue devoted to exploring honestly the declining numbers and resources across the Anglican Church. "Gone by

2040?" was the attention-grabbing headline. I have never heard our Church's paper prompt so much discussion. All through the holidays, people within my congregation—and across the church—reached out to share their thoughts on the issue. Challenged, shocked, alarmed, and depressed were a few of the adjectives used to describe how people felt.

I started 2020 feeling like I wasn't sure about my future, but that is nothing compared to the decades-long slump that one could argue is the life of the church. People have been saying for years that the mainline church is stuck—big time. It's not just the Canadian Anglican Church; it's the American Episcopal Church. It's the Lutherans, the Presbyterians, the Methodists, and various forms of United Church. Even statistics from the more evangelical spectrum of the Christian faith—long assumed to be bucking the trend and growing—suggest that decline is the norm across the board in organized religion.

"We just need to get young people in here," has been the anxious refrain for as long as I have been alive. Somehow, no matter how much we moan, though, the statistics keep getting more dire. We have pursued every sort of line of thinking to unstick ourselves: drums and PowerPoint and guitars in church, better signage to the washrooms, a robust social media presence, paid childcare for young families.

I am not saying that we shouldn't do these things. I am saying that all of them fall somewhere short of the goal of moving the dial on how the church does or doesn't connect with the world who isn't sitting in our pews on a Sunday morning. As journalist Giles Fraser unnervingly assesses the effectiveness of some of our efforts: "The Church feels like a gauche teenage boy going out to the pub deliberately to find a girlfriend, covering himself with cheap aftershave and rehearsing his unconvincing chat-up lines. It's all so cringe-worthy and needy."[1]

---

1 "The Church Is Abandoning Its Flock: The CofE's Great Leap Forward Will Cull Clergy and Abandon Parishioners," UnHerd, July 8, 2021, https://unherd.com/2021/07/the-church-is-abandoning-its-flock/.

I would liken our worries and our efforts of mainline Christianity to the church suffering from a problem with body image. I should know. I spent over half of my life wishing that my body were different from what it is. I couldn't look at myself and see the blessed and beautiful gift of my body. I could only see the extra pounds that I had bought into believing needed to be gone. This distorted body image eventually led to my being sick with an eating disorder.

I found healing for my eating disorder through the teachings of our faith. How ironic, then, to realize that I serve in a church that suffers from a bad body image too.

We might all be stressed out about how this church of ours is seen, affirmed, and valued in the life of the world, but we ourselves have had very little good to say ourselves about our own beauty or worth. We have been so concerned with feeling that the size of our congregations, the age of our parishioners, and the aesthetics of our outward appearance are lacking in significant ways that we have allowed these deficits to define us. How was I supposed to want to continue to be part of this thing when I myself was feeling so low and when the church as a whole has come to embody the story of how we are not relevant or popular, how we fundamentally don't measure up?

Surprising Affirmation

It was a strange and unnerving reality when the pandemic hit to have the wider society name the church, perhaps not as urgently needed, but definitely essential. St. George's had been livestreaming our worship services for years before COVID, so we were well situated to continue to gather people in prayer, even if it was online. However, as more and more of the world was shut down, we held our breath, waiting for the dictum that would say that our livestream skeleton crew would also be suspended. Instead, we were exempt from the stay-at-home order. The church was defined as essential.

How ironically strange. We spent most of 2020 unable to be together in person. This significant freedom we had so taken for granted, to be able to gather and practice our faith in peace, was snatched away from us. At the same time, the secular world around us was willing to acknowledge that continuing to provide public worship, even in a COVID-friendly way, was critically important. We had closed out the year wondering about the future of our denomination, and COVID certainly accelerated those worries and the potential for decline. We worried about finances. We worried about who would be coming back. We worried about the deaths that continued to mount in our parishes, particularly of our generous and committed senior generation.

In the midst of these worries was something else, though. The pandemic, the stay-at-home orders, and the definition of "essential" granted to our churches also provided much-needed focus on what we should have been asking all along: Why gather in Jesus's name at all? Why does the church even matter, beyond personal choice and individual preference? When we could no longer gather, what new things did we come to understand about why our gathering—in person or not—might actually be essential?

It was easy for us to answer those questions in terms of concrete forms of outreach: feeding the hungry and counseling the addicted, for example. St. George's people went to heroic lengths to keep our breakfast program offering its daily meal, to expand our feeding programs to include a Wednesday night takeout supper too, and to make sure that our Step Youth Resource Centre, for troubled young people in our community, could keep its doors open to teens in our city needing a safe place and a helping hand.

Worship and prayer were harder to put a finger on. "It feels like a lifeline," I heard countless people comment to me about our online worship. Even though our online numbers told a story of our people's need, we struggled to articulate why this awkward and new way of gathering felt so important. Our bishops in Ontario met together and decided that the offering of the Eucharist needed to be suspended while in-person worship was banned. If everyone couldn't receive the bread and wine at God's table, then nobody should receive it. Their decision might have been born out of compassion, but it suggested that this central sacrament of the church had no spiritual impact on the world beyond the immediate people who happened to make it out to our church buildings on a Sunday morning.

Surely, there is a connection between the church's steep decline and the coupling of our story of inadequacy with the story of how what we do only matters for ourselves. And yet, getting the story so wrong doesn't mean that the truer story isn't also there—about why the church matters, why it is essential and even urgent.

This truer story is easiest for me to name and claim when it comes through the flesh and blood of lived experience.

DISCUSSION QUESTIONS

1. What is your relationship to the mainline church? Are you newer to this tradition, or have you always been part of this expression of the church? Have you been part of other, more "popular" Christian traditions?

2. How has the story of decline in the mainline church affected you? Affected your relationship with the church?

3. What do you think of the church having a bad body image, unable to see its gifts and its beauty because it is too consumed with its own inadequacy?

4. Why do you think that worship was defined as "essential" during the pandemic? How does this designation challenge the church to better define who it is and why this matters?

CHAPTER 3

Urgent and Essential

The following two stories, on the surface, seem to be more about those easy, straightforward answers to the question of why the church matters: feeding ministries, corporal acts of care, the concrete call to cocreate with God a more just world. In truth, though, they point exactly to the heart of what it means to be a community gathered in worship and prayer, not to mention why we need to change our tune from those entrenched laments of shame and inadequacy toward a song that isn't just about us.

Story 1: High on a Tuesday Morning

It was a normal Tuesday morning several years before COVID. I arrived at the church just as our daily breakfast program was wrapping up and made my way from the parking lot to my office. We had been increasingly worried about what was happening in our breakfast program. More people were coming each morning. The guests kept skewing younger and younger. Our suspicion was that the combination of larger crowds and the disturbing reality that the drugs that were circulating were of a more potent and mind-bending sort led to a lot of aggression and vandalism. Michael had just come on staff at St. George's as our social justice and outreach director, and his work became focused toward first aid training in mental health and developing a mentor program for that early morning ministry. The mentors were to be people committed to nonviolent conflict management. They would also be friendly faces, people to sit at the tables with our guests, to talk with them and get to know them, to develop relationships.

On this particular Tuesday, the parking lot was swarming with people. The walkway up to the office was crowded too. Sitting on the half-step outside our memorial garden and blocking the way forward was a circle of people whom, from my early-forties vantage point, I labeled as kids. They weren't rude or aggressive when I needed to get by them, but they also did nothing to conceal the fact that they were shooting up. It was not even nine o'clock, and they were passing around needles and drugs openly on St. George's walkway.

I was shaken. It's not that I am especially surprised by drug use. I was shaken by how clear and unguarded their need was. You don't inject drugs into your arm on a Tuesday morning because you want to party. Shooting up on a Tuesday morning is not about having a good time or even making bad choices. It is about managing pain. It is about trying to stay alive when everything otherwise hurts too much. This group of kids was living in circumstances and engaging in behaviors that felt very far removed from me.

The easy thing to do is to pretend that the hurt and the destructive choices of others have nothing to do with us. The reality is that their pain and their chosen survival tactics reveal a brokenness in our society that we all need to take seriously; that, in fact, we all bear responsibility for; and that in a very real way *is* about all of us. What is our response to the revelation of profound pain?

As I took my steps through the circle of unguarded pain, a spark of an idea was born. The idea grew into the St. George's Step Centre, a resource center open to the young people of our city to provide counseling and support in response to the many and various needs youth are navigating. The need I saw was also seen by others. Suzanne became my fierce, generous, and compassionate partner in creating Step. She was the mover and shaker in growing the little seed of a thought into something real. Step opened in the fall of 2019, but my involvement in Step began that early Tuesday morning.

Story 2: Safe Water in Indigenous Communities

Many years before COVID, I made what felt like a straightforward suggestion to my congregation to devote some of our Christmas gift-giving that year toward raising funds for a well in a developing country.

"Let's give the gift of water," I enthused. St. David's Church in Orillia shared my enthusiasm. They are a congregation with a sense of adventure, and we certainly had fun trying new possibilities together. But quietly, at least half a dozen people voiced to me a troubling question in response.

"What about the people in Canada who don't have safe water? Shouldn't we be helping them?"

I was brought up in a small town in rural Ontario with a top-notch school system. Our teachers, I realize now, were on the leading edge of trends that wouldn't be codified for many years. I had a number of teachers who felt strongly about teaching us about Canada's colonial history. I knew that white Europeans had exploited and killed Indigenous people. And I knew that Indigenous children were forcibly taken away from their homes and put in residential schools. I knew they were subjected to horrible and inexplicable abuse while they were there.

I didn't connect the dots, though, between that history and the present-day reality of Canada. I turn on my tap, and water comes out. It is clean, it is safe, it comes in both cold and hot options. I barely think about it. I drink it, I bathe in it, I wash my food and my hands. I use it to flush our toilets. I squander and waste it.

There is a direct line between the project to "kill the Indian" that formed so much of Canada's history and the lack of drinking water in First Nation communities today. There is a direct line between the lack of drinking water and housing and food security in Indigenous communities today and the astronomical risk young Indigenous people face of dying by suicide. The line starts with severe trauma and systemic injustice. It takes us to remote Indigenous communities all across Canada that are not only continuing to process the loss of their children, but are also gravely, systemically, and cruelly underresourced in a country that is so rich it is impossible to justify why this would be. And it locates us in a place of despair so insidious and gripping that young people in these communities continually look at the world and see so much pain and so few opportunities that they take their own lives.

I have had the great privilege of working with and learning from archbishop Mark MacDonald, National Indigenous Archbishop of our Church, for the past ten-plus years. In the face of these youth suicides, this cruel injustice, the addiction and mental illness that reveals the ongoing trauma of this horrific history of stolen lands and stolen children, Archbishop Mark has an insight that he has shared on more than one occasion. "This is a spiritual crisis," he says.

These many and various crises Indigenous people are facing across our country all have a spiritual core. People have been disconnected from their language and their teachings. What's more, he noted that where they were experiencing real health and healing in their communities was in reconnecting to language and teachings that had been lost.

Of course, there is another component to that spiritual crisis, and that is in non-Indigenous Canada. We have lived as if we are somehow separate from Indigenous people and their concerns, as if we aren't shaped and diminished by this painful past too. We have pretended that we can be whole as a country—progressive and compassionate in the eyes of the world—when systemic injustice, systemic racism, systemic cruelty is not just part of our past, but very much imbedded in our present too. The issues faced in Indigenous Canada can't be compartmentalized into being just about Indigenous people.

Archbishop Mark has spoken truth to our Church and has continued to issue an urgent plea. Indigenous people are in the midst of a spiritual crisis. They are asking for the rest of the Church to join with them in empowering and equipping the Indigenous church to be part of how spiritual solutions are offered in response to these critical needs.

I think about this plea a lot. The rest of Canada has not collectively experienced genocide in the same way as Indigenous people, and in no way do I want to suggest that we have.

But I think about that group of young people shooting up on our church walkway on a Tuesday morning. I think about the pain revealed in their little circle huddled around their drugs. Addiction and mental illness are starkly visible in the downtown community that accesses our church's programs. And addiction, mental illness, and rising rates of anxiety and depression are an all-too familiar story behind middle-class doors across our communities too.

I think of the Black Lives Matter movement, whose pilot light was ignited in a major way in the spring of 2020 around the death of George Floyd. Clear trauma lines can be drawn, too, between the United States' history of slavery and the reality of disproportional poverty and incarceration in the Black people of North America today. I think of the terrible spiritual lie that led a whole nation believing themselves justified in owning and exploiting and abusing fellow human beings based on the color of their skin. And I think of the terrible spiritual lie of imagining today that we don't all bear responsibility for addressing the clearly documentable disadvantages that are built into people's lives now because of the color of their skin. It's not just that we bear responsibility, it is also that certainly we are all diminished by turning a blind eye.

I think of how COVID-19 made visible systemic racism, systemic neglect of those in our care facilities, and the true price of gross economic inequality. And I think of the environmental crisis, that has been banging on our doors for decades while we have mostly acted paralyzed to answer, that isn't going away, and not responding to it is increasingly putting us all in peril.

Archbishop Mark named the interconnected crises in Indigenous communities as a fundamentally spiritual crisis—a disconnection from key spiritual truths. But all of us have become disconnected from who we are: beloved of God and biologically/spiritually/emotionally connected to one another, bound to one another and to all life on this planet, whether we like it or not.

What If It's Actually Connected?

Indigenous leaders of our church have named their community's crisis with clarity and courage as being a disconnection from unalterable spiritual truths. We need to listen and consider this truth more broadly.

What if the disconnection from spiritual truths is the source of crisis? The flourishing of addiction, depression, anxiety, mental illness, and suicide in our communities is all rooted in spiritual crisis. The melting glaciers and rising global temperatures, the hemming and hawing about whether climate change is real and whether it's more important to save the fossil fuel industry or if we should embrace change that gives the possibility of our lives on this planet continuing, is a spiritual crisis. The endless pursuit of self-realization, of ricocheting between believing that I'm not good enough and also that I should do whatever I want in order to be happy, and the sad truth that both of these pursuits leave me feeling empty and anxious is a spiritual crisis too.

What about me and my little life? What about all the people who are part of our churches, who have had their hearts broken, who have come face to face with the fragility of their lives, who know loss and love and the struggle to pick up the pieces when everything falls apart? I don't think that Jesus is the quick and easy miracle balm that just needs to be applied to our bruised souls. It's not that if people don't believe in Jesus they will end up addicted to drugs and become climate change deniers. Nor am I suggesting that if our world just woke up and found Jesus then mental illness and global warming would be eradicated.

But Archbishop Mark speaks truth, and it is truth that is born out of the crucible of immense pain and suffering: When we really open our eyes, we see a world of vast, intimate, intricate, and multidimensional relationship. We also see all kinds of damage and destruction as our human family continually attempts to live outside of that relationship. The relationships in which we actually exist and have life do need to be reclaimed, named, and offered with confidence and urgency to a world in need.

If we believe—and we do claim to believe this—that God really is concerned with the health and healing of the whole earth, not merely the survival of the institutional church, what is the church doing if it isn't on board with proclaiming the message of God's saving help for us all? And if we are on board with that, surely we also have to be on board with claiming that faith matters, and it matters urgently. It matters for me because it matters for all of us.

My crisis happened to coincide with the world's pandemic and with questions that had long been in front of the church. All of this succeeded in putting everything on the table—up for negotiation—in a way that allowed us to see what communal faith actually is, why it matters, and how it can be a force for reconnection in the midst of our disconnected and disjointed lives. That's what I want to serve. I want to be part of a faith that connects our fractured lives back to what is true and real.

DISCUSSION QUESTIONS

1. Archbishop Mark MacDonald names the crises around addiction and suicide in Indigenous communities as a "spiritual crisis" because they are founded in a disconnection from key spiritual truths. How can we see other areas of pain and brokenness in our world as being, at their core, a "spiritual crisis"?

2. "The relationships in which we actually exist and have life do need to be reclaimed, named, and offered with confidence and urgency to a world in need." How might this be a starting point for understanding the urgency of our faith?

CHAPTER 4

The Songs That Are Too Big

Many clergy get into ministry because we have experienced the saving power of faith as a point of reconnection and healing across the fractures in our own lives. But the work of ministry and the life of the church can easily feel far away from that starting motivation. Before I could find any sort of way back to joy in ministry, I had to get more honest about how real the disconnect had become and how fragile it had left me.

Where Is the Exit?

"I haven't heard from you since March!" one parishioner said accusingly when I called to check in. "You never called; I thought you didn't care," another commented bitterly. "Nobody reaches out; nobody is there to pray with us or ask how we are," a third complained.

These particular criticisms were lodged at me, back to back to back in the week between Christmas and New Year's Eve of 2020—a week that I should have had off but instead used for catching up on phone calls and pastoral care matters. I also opened an angry email on Boxing Day. A parishioner wrote to express her fury about the music selection for our Christmas Eve livestream. Our services were shut down for in-person worship by pandemic protocols just two days before Christmas, and our cantor for Christmas Eve broke her back on the morning of the 24th. Brad, our director of music, and I had done our level best to pull something together at the last minute. This angry email just about did me in.

I had started 2020 in a bad state but mostly in denial about how much ministry was not working for me. Over the course of the COVID year, things went from bad to much, much worse. The obvious stressors were just the tip of the iceberg: continually adapting to shifting ministry protocols, the added responsibilities of administration, email and technological drudgery that goes with worshipping together online, the big empty space of our sanctuary, the deaths in our parish that we couldn't properly mourn, and adapting to the awkwardness of leading worship to a camera and trying desperately, as if my life depended on it, to remember and visualize the real people on the other side of that camera. Beyond these soul-destroying concerns, there were personnel matters and COVID-adjacent stresses across our parish with which I felt desperately ill equipped to deal. And there were the criticisms that anxious and unhappy and isolated people at home kept lobbing at me and the rest of the leadership.

It was a recipe for a frantic unhappiness that was taking hold of me in my life as a parish priest. I began to evaluate my gifts in a way that I had not for almost two decades. I had long considered myself to be a borderline extrovert. Although I am naturally quiet, I have felt energized by my leadership in the church—crowded services, busy coffee hours, long conversations with a group Bible study. I can go into a Sunday morning service feeling tired and out of sorts from whatever kid or dog was up in the middle of the night, and I can come out feeling rejuvenated.

With in-person worship suspended, though, and with the daily routine of physical person-to-person interaction moved to the qualitatively different experience of online Zoom gatherings, I started to realize how much of my life existed way outside of my real comfort zone. I am not an extrovert at all. I am an introvert who craves alone time like I crave oxygen. I can happily retreat to a couch with a pile of books or to a running route and the sanctuary of my ear buds blocking out the rest of the world. Not only that, but I have also realized that I am not a natural leader. It is not my default to be either in charge or in the limelight. The most comfortable and life-giving place for me is as a back-up singer in a band or in the alto section of a choir. All of my leadership and people skills are adaptations: I have been asked to do certain work, and I have been able to develop the skill sets necessary to be able to do that work.

I was not the only one wondering in 2020 if there might be an escape hatch. As long ago as 2010, the *New York Times* was reporting that "members of the clergy now suffer from obesity, hypertension and depression at rates higher than most Americans. In the last decade, their use of antidepressants has risen, while their life expectancy has fallen. Many would change jobs if they could."[1]

Before the pandemic, clergy were already the focal point of highly anxious systems. The church has faced questions of decline and survival for decades, and all too often, clergy are tasked with Messiah-like expectations of bailing out the sinking ship and saving the institutional church. When things go well, they get put on a pedestal; when things don't go as well as hoped, they get blamed. Either way, mental health of our clerics is often the fall guy. And it's not just in Christian communities either. Rabbi Joel Meyers summarized in that same *New York Times* article the stress that many of us experience—pandemic or not: "Rabbis today are expected to be the C.E.O. of the congregation and the spiritual guide, and never be out of town if somebody dies. And reply instantly to every e-mail."

When the article "Six Reasons Your Pastor Is About to Quit" was published in the summer of 2020, numerous friends forwarded it to me, along with the tired recognition that the piece reflected something of their own experience. The article named the uncertainty and anxiety of the pandemic and postpandemic church as factors in their weariness. But maybe more significantly, it outed congregations for their increased expectations on their pastors, the workload that never stops expanding, and the criticisms that keep coming, no matter how much time and effort the people in leadership expend.[2]

---

1   Paul Vitello, "Taking a Break from the Lord's Work," *New York Times*, August 1, 2010, https://www.nytimes.com/2010/08/02/nyregion/02burnout. html.
2   Thom S. Rainer, "Six Reasons Your Pastor Is about to Quit," *Church Answers* (blog), August 31, 2020, https://churchanswers.com/blog/ six-reasons-your-pastor-is-about-to-quit/.

One friend and colleague shared with me the struggle of "dealing with my own depression and self-care and working to find a balance between being there for my parishioners and caring for myself. The normal ways in which I would reach out and connect with people are so restricted that I often feel quite ineffective in my pastoral work." Another noted that the constantly shifting public health protocols of COVID demanded a superhuman output of energy, while the things that normally feed us in ministry were no longer part of the package. But she also identified the core problem of our work as being bigger than just a pandemic. Perhaps COVID is actually revealing what the *New York Times* article suggested has long been the case. She told me, "The challenge at the best of times is that the work is boundaryless. There is always more work to do than a normal day will hold."

My friend Brian could see how much I was struggling. He suggested I call together a circle of supportive friends to talk through the difficulties I was feeling. I didn't exactly see how that would help, but I have learned that Brian's advice is worth taking, and so I reached out to Scott, Kevin, and Cheryl to join Brian and me on a Zoom call. They were representative of so many others I am blessed to know have my back, even when I'm not at my best. Admitting that I am overwhelmed and in need of help is a tough thing for me. But it's an important place to start in terms of finding any sort of truth.

A Taste for Too-Big Songs

I get cravings for music the way I get cravings for salt and vinegar chips. A song or an album comes into my head, and my auditory taste buds salivate until I get to hear it. That's how Throwing Copper by the band Live came to be on my playlist during this time of struggle.

Around the time of the album's release in 1994, Live was the hottest band on the planet. My dear friend Kira and I went to see them a number of times, each occasion having its own chapter's worth of adventure. We greeted each album release with awe and reverence, pouring over lyrics and packing our mixtapes with their songs.

Throwing Copper was Live's third album and the one that launched them into mass popularity. Listening to it now as an adult, I can say (with a touch of regret) that the album doesn't hold up. The melodies are as comforting and reassuring to me as a warm bath. My auditory taste buds thrill to hear it again. But it also undeniably has some inexcusably horrible lyrics. I'm not sure there could be anything more pretentious than a male alt-rocker warbling lines about placentas and angels in all seriousness.

My daughter, Cecilia, was in the car with me when one of the songs from the album popped up. This one—"White, Discussion"—was not a hit, but it had seemed especially meaningful to me when I was about their age. They politely asked that we turn off the music and talk instead. When I questioned Cecilia on their opinion of my beloved song, they did a piercingly accurate impression of Ed Kowalczyk's overly intense falsetto.

Cecilia's laughing and my cringing aside, I couldn't help but to join in loudly singing along with each song and to feel both happy about and nostalgic for my sixteen-year-old self. I'm glad that my coming-of-age years were accompanied by an overly intense falsetto and lyrics that tried to say too much.

Listening now, I hear the all-consuming crushes I had on boys who I was sure would never notice me, as well as the awkward break-ups and rejections I had to negotiate in that dance of raging emotions and mostly unrequited love that defines the teenage years for so many of us. I hear my first love, Shawn, the one who loved me back, and all the road trips between his house and mine as we became each other's primary witness to the joys, worries, and choices of growing up. I hear the confusion of navigating female friendships, ever shifting alliances between various girlfriends as we sought to bare our hearts to one another and claim soul mates, as well as assert what little amounts of power we could over one another. I hear my own self-righteous anger about injustices I was beginning to understand in the world and perceived injustices I myself thought I was experiencing. I hear my confused relationship with my parents, sure that they couldn't possibly understand me and also just as sure that their eternally welcoming embrace could fix any ill. I hear that barely-beneath-the-surface dawning knowledge of mortality that is so much a part of being a teenager; I hear the teenaged insistence that those boundaries of our own mortality be tested with varying degrees of foolishness. And maybe most especially, I hear a spirituality and sense of call that was just being awakened in me. The world, I was sure, was a broken place, and we were a misguided people, and also I was full of wonder and intensity and hope and passion and knew more than anything that I needed to be the kind of person to make a difference.

There isn't anything carefree about being a teenager. It's all growing body parts and out-of-control chemical reactions taking over our bodies and trying to process large quantities of information about the world and negotiating a variety of possible identities in order to figure out who we are and who we will be.

I'm glad that I had music that tried to say too much and songs that were way too big to help me negotiate those realities. Lightning Crashes yearns to name in the tragedy and seemingly randomness of life an overarching meaning, that out of our mistakes and failures comes new possibility, that our patterns of death and life are fundamentally connected to one another, that death is needed in order to make room for something new. The symphony of emotions that make it so hard to negotiate love and friendship and that lead me to seek whatever else may be out there have all been felt before. My perceived aloneness is just that: a perception.

In these lyrics, even all of these years later, I hear the awkward articulation of a notion I would come to believe with the entirety of my body, mind, and spirit. The emotional and spiritual journey of one little person, one little person like me, is connected to the work of healing the world.

Trying to Say Everything

My taste for too-big songs has only gotten stronger in adulthood. Every week, sometimes every day, pandemic or not, I get to invite a community of faith into all of the too-big songs that we offer in the average worship service: songs about life and death, crosses and suffering, sin and redemption, principalities, powers, the shedding of blood, and the promise of resurrection. Every time we bless the bread and wine of communion, we invite the whole congregation to join in singing words that try to say everything:

Holy, holy, holy, Lord God of hosts
Heaven and earth are full of your glory.
Hosanna in the highest.
Blessed is the one who comes in the name of the Lord.
Hosanna in the highest.

In some important sense, the Sanctus (as we call these words) speaks to the teenager in each of us, right through all of the things we think we have figured out and into the vulnerable, searching place still inside us. We are invited to lay our souls bare before God and get honest about our own need and brokenness. It is all getting gathered and raised up into this one song that insists that the ugliness and pain and failings of our lives are not separate from God's glory and are even now being claimed and redeemed by God's love and light. Many of us will cross ourselves in the second part of this song, "Blessed is the one . . .". For Christians, that blessed one is Jesus, our path and promise. We cross ourselves as a sign of our invitation to share in that identity. God's name is written on my heart too. I get to be part of how Jesus is still present and leading among us. Hosanna in the highest!

The best thing about our church's too-big songs is that I don't ever sing them alone. This, ironically, became especially apparent when we were livestreaming our services to an empty sanctuary. The claim that all of the company of heaven joins in with us when we sing felt viscerally real in a surprising way. That moment of worship in particular, the Sanctus, is a "thin place," a place where the veil between this life and the next flutters perceptibly. I swear I can hear more voices joining in than the number merely represented in the visible congregation before me. The sanctuary might feel empty, but it also feels full.

Surely the complaints fired my way in that post-Christmas email were born out of that same instinct I had in reconnecting to the songs of my younger self. COVID or not, the strongest opinions I hear voiced in any church I have ever served have been about music. We look to our songs to keep us safe in scary times. We look to our songs to shelter us in the warm embrace of nostalgia. We look to our songs to soothe us in our exhaustion, fear, uncertainty, failure, rage, grief, and disappointment. We look to our songs to express things that words alone can't say.

It's only when I myself am feeling so depleted that I can't see that the complaints were only minimally about me. Mostly what they revealed was how much common ground we share—both in our feelings of extreme vulnerability and where we ultimately seek solace.

Sometimes It Starts with a Sigh

There were a number of stops along the road back to saying yes to God's call in my life once again, when everything was suddenly put on the table, when who I was and how I was spending my life was just one of many things being called into question. You will hear some of these moments sprinkled throughout this book. I would love to share with you a dramatic story of sudden conversion marking the start of the road back. Lightning bolts from heaven, messages written in the sky, or even just a quiet voice speaking to me in the dead of night all would have been welcome ways of hearing from God.

Often the turning point on our journeys doesn't start with a message, it starts with a sigh. I think about Jesus asking his little band of disciples if they were going to leave him. He had made a lot of controversial statements about himself and his relationship to God, and the crowds who had been so enamored with his miracles, particularly the feeding of the masses with just a few loaves and fish, felt they couldn't continue on with him and his radical ideas. Peter spoke up in response to Jesus's question: "Where else will we go? You have the words of eternal life" (John 6:68). It was not a roaring endorsement, but sometimes that moment of resignation is all we have.

That was me in my circle of friends admitting that I wasn't managing. I wasn't less stuck; I was more stuck. But where else was I going to go? God wasn't giving me any escape hatches. Nine months out from that busted trip to Jerusalem and my frantic realization that I wasn't going to get to go anywhere, all I had was that sigh of resignation. I would have liked a more dramatic turning point back to reaffirming ministry, but at least it was a starting point.

From there, I had these people who were willing to be with me in my honest admission of failing. And connected to that little representation of community were these too-big songs.

My favorite part in revisiting the well-worn songs from my youth is the realization that I'm still that same person that I was at sixteen, needing songs that will try desperately to say everything, even if that attempt inevitably fails. My heart still pulses with love that feels risky and uncontainable. I know the cost of love and the truth of death in a different way, and I also know how new life keeps bubbling up in the most surprising places. I worry about politics and climate change and church growth and decline and being those arms of unconditional welcome for my own kids. I want them to feel seen and understood, and I am all too aware of how I sometimes fail them. My mixtapes of the nineties are gone, and my car playlists now include music of all kinds, with a favoring of those that are too big and still try to say too much.

Here's the thing about all of those too-big songs that I still love and, more importantly, that I still need. They are connected to my identity as a priest. My identity as a priest is not a nice, neat, direct line to God; it is shaped in the life of community, in a circle of people. Sometimes all that circle of people seems capable of doing is radiating my own pain back to me, like in those angry outbursts at the height of the pandemic. But also it's in that circle of people that we can see the truth: our prayer and sacred stories, our acts of service and sometimes our angry emails are all bound up in this wild, desperate attempt to give voice to a song that is always too big—about the things that we most want and need and desperately seek. We want to be held and loved. We want to be seen; we want our lives to matter.

We want to connect with what is real.

DISCUSSION QUESTIONS

1. What are the too-big songs in your life? What is the music that you turn to that speaks to the core of who you are and what matters to you?

2. What are your thoughts on clergy burnout?

3. For members of our congregations, do you think about the health and wellness of your pastors? Is caring for them part of how your church attends to its overall wellness?

4. For fellow clergy, how do you cope with the demands of the job?

5. Martha says that there are words in our worship services that "speak to the teenager in each of us, that vulnerable and searching place inside each of us." She also says that, in worship, we never sing alone. How do you experience the words and songs of worship allowing you to be honest, vulnerable and real?

6. How does worship allow you to connect to the greater communion of the church—those in other times and places from us?

CHAPTER 5

"Martha, We Are the Church"

I was messaging with my friend Matthew. We were frustrated. We were frustrated by the church. The reasons for this frustration aren't especially important, but the fact of our frustration is worth highlighting. You can't spend a significant amount of time connected to the church without running up against the hair-tearing, sleep-stealing, insanity-making frustration of trying to live as this vast global community of faith with a whole bunch of people that we don't necessarily like, understand, or agree with.

We were talking about leaving, about fighting for the change we wanted to see and why. "There is a reality of the church that is worth fighting for," I commented, trying to rally my own energy for continuing on.

"Martha," he replied immediately, "We are the church."

The Problem Is the Christians

I participated as a workshop leader at the New Story Festival in Austin, Texas, in 2019. Nadia Bolz-Weber was the keynote speaker. She started by saying that she was struggling with being a Christian. Her problem, she clarified, wasn't Jesus. Her problem was the Christians. Her problem was all the crappy ways that Christians use Jesus to support their own violent, selfish, divisive, and destructive agendas. She theorized that most people don't fall out of faith because of Jesus. They fall out of faith because of Jesus's followers. It's a sentiment that resonates with many. In our year of collective upheaval, when I wasn't sure I wanted to continue with the church, it was a sentiment that resonated with me too.

But there are those songs, the ones that are too big and the ones that kept me tethered to the life of worship and to my identity as a priest. And there is this truth too—awkward and unwelcome as it is at times. "We are the church," just as Matthew said. There isn't any way of leaving this thing, as much as we might want to.

"Where else would we go?" Peter sighed to Jesus.

The reality both Matthew and Peter are pointing to is that we're infected with one another. "Infection" is a concept that, at the best of times, has negative connotations and is representative of all that we fear, especially in the middle of a pandemic. It is unnerving to our super-sanitized lives to realize that no amount of handwashing can change the fact that my body is constantly ingesting the water and air molecules that have been ingested and expelled by the people around me. Lockdown living was a response to the reality of just how connected we really are, and even when we did our best to stay away from one another, the relentless progress of COVID across our globe was only ever slowed, not stopped.

This biological truth is also connected to a religious truth. Just as our physical bodies are literally made up of the life of the world, so the life of our fellow Christians is our life.

Nadia's insight about how hard it can be to believe because of the nastiness of the Christians is certainly true. Being infected with one another doesn't sound great. But not liking it doesn't make it any less real; not liking it doesn't mean that we get to opt out of how this world is set up to biologically and spiritually bind us to one another.

Here's the truth for me. My identity as a priest is totally and completely and inextricably connected to the church, the community of Jesus's followers. I don't always like that, but it is always true. I wonder if there's a way for it to be both true and a choice. It's true that I'm a priest, but can I also choose it? It's true that we're infected with each other, but can we opt to live as if this is a good and life-giving thing after all?

To Lift Up

As a priest, my job description is simple. My job is to lift up.

It's an image that comes from the Eucharist, from the gathering around God's table to share bread and wine in Jesus's name.

The priest lifts up the bread and the wine and says, "The gifts of God's creation and the work of human hands," and asks that in this bread and wine we see and receive and even ingest God's promise to meet us in the brokenness of our lives and the mess that is this world.

It's symbolic of the entire work to which I am called. In meeting people in hospital rooms and at their death beds, in responding to emails about mental health crises and fundraising ideas, in leading Bible studies and asking people to serve on committees, in all of the administrative and financial details that go into providing the support for feeding programs and worship opportunities, in listening through the week to the conversations around me so that I can preach in some way to the burning cares on people's hearts, I am attending to the promise of God meeting us here in the mess of our lives. I am lifting up that promise in all of those little nitty-gritty encounters in the hope, in the belief, that our lives are strengthened, healed, blessed by being tuned in to the nearness of God's love.

My husband, Dan, is a priest also. When he was little, he would make his sister play church with him, spreading out pretend bread and wine on a pretend altar and going through the motions that he saw the priests of his church doing. Many of my colleagues report similar inklings of vocation from their childhood play.

That was never me. I didn't see this for myself. I hope to one day retire from church leadership and sing in the choir. I don't expect to be the kind of person who will look for opportunities to preach and preside at services into my later years. I look forward to participating in our worship with someone else doing the literal and public work of lifting up.

But what I do believe is core to my identity—and perhaps the reason why God tapped me on the shoulder for this particular work—is paying attention to, naming and claiming, the power of God's love drawing near, and revealed, in our human life. What's more, I believe that this naming and claiming is essential to our knowing joy and hope. I believe this is the starting point for how we then respond to the brokenness of our world. I believe that this personal faith—God at work in actual flesh-and-blood human persons—is at the heart of what it is to be a church, why the church matters, and how God might be able to use the church, the community of faith, to reveal healing and to pour out love into our world.

Nadia Bolz-Weber was speaking truth. Jesus's followers can be terrible. They can screw up, they can hurt and maim, and they can be the reason why people lose their faith altogether. I could write another couple of books about all of the ways that I, and people I love, have been hurt by the institution of the church and by the people who make up our communities of faith.

The cold, hard truth, the wretched truth of the matter, is that the opposite is also true. We need one another. We need one another to know and love Jesus. We need the community of faith and the stories of how God has been at work in actual, real lives—not just our own, but others' too—in order to love and serve God. Not just that, but we are the community of faith. We are the stories of how God has been at work in the world. "Martha," Matthew said, "We are the church."

COVID-19 succeeded in putting everything on the table; stripping away so many of the patterns, the norms, the taken-for-granted gifts of our lives; and forcing us to ask what really matters now. Not being together in worship begged the question for us of whether gathering in Jesus's name even matters. And with everything on the table in my own life, the thing I was left with was just this: the promise, the experience, in me and most especially in you that we need to learn to see the nudging of that curtain that so easily covers our lives to attend again to how God is at work in us, at work in us with love.

"I'm Tired"

Because I have always been part of the declining church, I have also been subjected to any number of programs and trends in the church that are supposed to save us. Some of these offerings blatantly promise numerical growth; others make vaguer promises but are also speaking of transformation and vitality for the institutional church.

The desperate desire to save, grow, and transform the church marks a lot of what weighs on the minds and hearts of parish leaders, the expectations that are placed on us, and what creates the most anxiety in our work. Our professional development opportunities tend to be either focused on corralling us into leading these new ways of being the church or on offering us models of self-care to recover from all the stress of always trying to get our communities to become something different from what they currently are. In a breakout session in one such professional development day for clergy, one of my colleagues expressed his fatigue at what was being shared by our charismatic presenter.

"I'm tired," he shared with weariness. "I'm tired of being given yet another hypothetical vision of what the church should be."

Truth. The church is like me when I was so locked into obsessing about wanting smaller thighs or fewer inches around my waist. I became completely disconnected from being able to see, love, and value the body I actually had. Much of the mainline church in which we serve is so concerned with institutional decline that all it can see is its own faults and failings; all it can wish is to be and look like something other than what it is.

The church is also like me in the eye of the pandemic hurricane wishing that there was another option for who I could be.

My colleague's words hit me like a punch in the gut. I know that dead-end road all too well. Not only am I not interested in a hypothetical vision of what the church should be, I realized that there is no hypothetical vision of what I could, should, might be either. There is just the realization that when it's all on the table, somehow or other, I'm still being asked to lift something up. Somehow the place where there is life is in the ability to see, give thanks for, and bless what actually is.

Ultrarealism

The questions of identity and the search for what is real began for me on a Friday morning just before COVID was declared a global pandemic. I was out running and had just nicely gotten into the rhythm that I can only find after I have a few miles under my belt.

Running is partly about physical strength and preparation. But it is mostly about getting into the right head space. It is easy as a runner to expend large amounts of energy and anxiety worrying about what might happen or wishing that things could be different from what they are when you have twenty, thirty, or forty kilometers stretching in front of you. If we instead train our minds to focus on what is actually happening and how we really feel, a new sort of freedom opens up.

I might get freaked out about how my breathing is uneven. I might feel despair about the spitting rain outside and how slowly the first kilometer seems to have gone when I still have twenty-nine kilometers to go. But while these things about breathing and rain and mileage might be true, I can choose to note that my leg muscles feel strong, the rain is refreshing, and I have the great privilege of being able to run. I am not just not dying, I am not just safe and okay; I am running, and it feels good. In endurance sports, this mental act of seeing, accepting, and embracing the reality of any situation is called ultrarealism.

"I'm doing it!" my friend Sarah uses as her power statement. It's an ultrareal power statement. It's not the power of positive thinking. It's a statement of fact. For all of the worry or uncertainty or reluctance that we might feel about putting on our shoes and tackling some mileage, here we actually can find ourselves— out running. We are out here. And we are doing this.

Ultrarealism is not unlike the famous serenity prayer: "God grant me the courage to change the things that I can, the serenity to accept the things I can't, and the wisdom to know the difference." There is much about the circumstances of a run that I can't change or control, and within all that isn't shaped and dictated by me is the choice to keep one foot going in front of the other. Somewhere in the letting go and the choosing anyway is a wild and surprising joy.

With all of the questions about the institutional church before us, particularly in terms of its well-documented numerical decline, and with the acceleration of that decline because of the pandemic, we can be guaranteed that the offerings for what might save the church, what might remake and transform us into vital and meaningful offerings in the lives of the general population again are going to be steeply on the rise. There are going to be many opportunities in the coming months and years to consider how to draw people to the community of faith, to be followers of Jesus.

But I suspect there is somewhere else we should start. There is a starting place of seeing, accepting, and embracing our actual reality. That starting place is life-giving. My utter conviction is that to discover what is life-giving in the community of faith for me and for us is also viscerally connected to how the community of faith can be, and actually is, life-giving for the world. It starts with us. Not just me, not just you, but us. "Reality is that which, when you stop believing in it, doesn't go away," says Philip K. Dick.[1] Here is what doesn't go away: the bonds of relationship between us have no override button. That is the actual situation, the ultrareal of our lives. Whether we like it or not, the world is set up for us to be biologically and spiritually and emotionally infected with and connected to one another.

This connection doesn't go away: God is already at work in this massive, inextricably infected reality of what it is to be alive in this particular universe. Maybe what we need to do most urgently is to get better at training our eyes to see, accept, and embrace this unalterable truth.

That's my job as a priest. To lift up that truth. But the reality is that priestly ministry isn't just mine, it's a ministry that is of the whole community—I just happen to be the one at St. George's, St. Catharines, who is often there at the altar physically elevating the bread and wine along with these words of promise. I do that so that we all can do that. So that we can all strengthen and train our muscles to be able to perceive better what is actually going on.

---

1 Dick, quoted in Fitzgerald, *The Comeback Quotient*, 1.

That is where we go from here, to this starting place. This is a book about the church, the community of faith—not who we should be, or could be, or must want to be. It's a book lifting up who we actually are so we can see the stories of the God who meets us here. It's a book inviting us to accept our identity as part and parcel of how we know God's goodness and then to embrace that identity as we realize that even as we might be stuck with one another, we can also choose one another. Our lives are bound together, and also God meets us right in the thick of that binding—in the joy and pain, the heartbreak and wonder, of how we love and serve and mess up and try to live and eventually die.

That's why we gather—to be better tuned in to what God is doing in our lives. Tuning in to this truth matters to us in ways that are urgent and consequential because it is exactly this—to be in relationship with one another and in relationship with God—for which we are created.

And it's not just about us either. The church isn't just about us. The blessings of God multiply. God meets us here in the nitty-gritty of our lives, not just that we ourselves may know how we are loved, but how we can be part of how the world may know God's love too.

It Was Hunger

Caitlyn is a young woman who came to St. George's because she thought she would try Anglicanism. She liked our website, and when she spoke to me and the other clergy, she felt comfortable with us. Although she loved the church immediately and got involved right away, she never came up for communion.

"To be clear," she said later in an interview we did at the church in our online Dessert & Dish feature, "I knew that I was allowed to come up for communion. I knew that I was welcome. People made sure I was invited. But I hated that part of the service. I would feel nauseous when we got to that part. It just made me feel so uncomfortable."

COVID-19 threw the church into lockdown, and we had to get used to worshipping predominantly online, not in person. For the first few months, the wider Church of which we are part mandated that we not celebrate communion in our services.

In April Caitlyn had a dream. She walked into a room where there was a big table, and a lot of people were at the table eating bread, talking, and sharing things. Jesus was at the table. Caitlyn commented that it didn't look like Jesus in the artwork that the Christian church often favors. He had no halo. He looked like an ordinary person, although Caitlyn knew who it was. He invited her to come to the table, but she stayed watching in the doorway. She watched others come through the door and take their place at the table. The table kept expanding to make room for more and more people.

Caitlyn couldn't go sit down, and she couldn't tear herself away. Jesus then called her by name and invited her again to sit down. Finally, she was able to leave the doorway and take a seat. She discovered as she sat down that she was ravenously hungry, that she couldn't wait to eat.

"I only had that dream once when I was asleep," she shared later. "But I think about it all the time when I'm awake. It's like I keep dreaming it, although awake. And the hunger in that dream felt totally real. It didn't feel like a dream."

Caitlyn became anxious during that first COVID lockdown about getting back to in-person worship services. "What if we never go back?" she asked. "What if I die before we go back? What if I never get to have communion at St. George's?" This part of the service that had been so incredibly awkward for her, so awkward that it made her feel nauseous, became the part of worship that she had a burning need in which to participate.

On September 13, 2020, we were able to open our doors again for in-person worship for a couple of months before the second wave shut us down again. Caitlyn was signed up for the first service of the day. "It's now my favorite part of the service," she reflected several months later. "I just wait for that part of the service. But I don't feel, like, warm and glowy afterwards," she said.

"It's not nice. I feel urgently hungry when I come up. I thought it was nausea, but it was actually hunger."

In that dream, Caitlyn took communion with outstretched hands and named her own hunger and need. Such is the reality of what the church is. Right now. It's a table. Everything is on it. Our whole lives are laid bare before God—our fear, our nausea, our reluctance, our blindness, and our hunger. Right now, Jesus is calling us to find the seat that has already been created for us, to be welcomed, to eat, and to meet the God who comes right here exactly to meet us.

DISCUSSION QUESTIONS

1. "Martha, we are the church." How does it shift our perspective on our relationship to the church to realize that, like it or not, the church is us?

2. How do you experience the church's relationship with decline? Do you connect to Martha's experience of the church's constant focus on trying to be different from what it actually is? Is there freedom in "not another hypothetical version of what the church might be"?

3. Consider Caitlyn's dream of the table and of Jesus calling her to find her place there. How is this a vision for the church? Is there another image for the church that resonates for you?

II

Not Another Hypothetical Version of What the Church Could Be

CHAPTER 6

I Had Another Plan

I wanted to be a lawyer.

I was an ambitious teenager, and I thought I had my life figured out. I had my high school course of study set. I had top grades and a slew of extracurricular activities (mostly in music and student council—no athletics for this bookworm!), so I was hopeful I could get a good scholarship and work my way toward law school.

What I didn't anticipate doing was falling in love with Jesus.

It's not a turn of phrase that resonates with everyone, but it's an accurate description of what happened. I had been going to church my whole life, mostly because I felt that was something that good people did and because it made my mom happy. When I was fifteen, a bossy and passionate priest, Ed, came to our church. I am not sure how I would relate to his tactics now, but he had no reservations about lecturing from the pulpit about what the shape of Christian faith should look like. We should read our Bibles, we should pray for one another, we should pay attention to all of the little details of sign and symbol in our liturgy that tell in ways much deeper than words what we really believe.

It was the combination of reading the Bible and tuning in more intentionally to worship that set the stage. I fell in love with this radical, brave, witty, compassionate Jesus and with the liturgy that, at its heart, is structured in order to reveal to us that he is not some long-dead hero of the faith. He lives in us and is still meeting us on the rocky roadways of life. The problem with falling in love with Jesus was the competing claim on my heart: I wanted to be a lawyer. But I had this nagging feeling that I was supposed to be a priest.

I was a really serious teenager. But I was also a teenager. My friends didn't go to church. My boyfriends weren't Christian.

My friends and I talked about everything, as teenagers do, but mostly we just goofed around. We pined after our crushes, we carefully curated our lockers to present a picture of our beautiful and carefree lives filled with friends, boys, and attractive clothing. We wondered how to get the guys we liked to like us back, and we sometimes lost interest when they finally did.

My parents were committed churchgoers, as were my grandparents, but I knew all of them would struggle to understand why my faith could interrupt my perfectly good plan of being a lawyer. People who were too enthusiastic about religion were viewed with suspicion by every single person who was close to me.

It wasn't just a problem of what others saw in me, though. It was also what I wanted for myself. I wanted to make money. I wanted all of the signs of worldly success. I wanted a big house, nice cars, fun vacations, and the admiration of others. Being a priest in a church didn't fit any of the bills I had set up in my mind's eye about who I was or where my life was going. But that nagging feeling wouldn't go away.

So I bargained. I didn't need quite so much of the worldly success. I could be a lawyer and work for legal aid. I could be a lawyer and save the environment—represent Greenpeace or something. I could be a lawyer for the first part of my adult life, make a comfortable (not decadent) living, and then I could work for the church—for free, even—if I could just be a lawyer for the first thirty years of my professional life. If God could give me until about fifty-five, then I would become a priest.

I don't remember the moment of giving in. I also don't remember what the conversations were like—with my parents, grandparents, brother, and my best friends Mendi and Brandy, Jeanine and Kira. There was no turning point. The knowledge that I couldn't spend all of those years trying to be one thing when I knew I was something else—someone else—eventually overtook me. By the time I turned sixteen, the people closest to me knew that law was off the table. I knew it too. Disappointing as it was to admit this, I knew I wasn't a lawyer. I was a priest.

Not Giving Up but Seeing What Is Really There

"Isn't ultrarealism just giving up?" my friend Kate asked when I described the premise. "Are we just saying that there's nothing more we can do as a church? Just quietly go off and die?"

She asked an important question. Because the mainline church has been so defined by its own decline, it is easy to suppose that when we talk about getting real about who we are, the "real" looks like admitting that the church we love and serve is dying. There isn't anything particularly hopeful or life-giving about waiting around to die.

Here's the thing. I resisted becoming a priest because I wanted to put my time and energy elsewhere. In the end, I couldn't sign up for a life of waiting around to finally retire and be able to be who I really am. I would say that the mainline church has gotten itself trapped in putting its time, energy, and worry into preserving, propping up, and trying to save something other than who we really are.

This book started with my own questions about identity, about whether my work as a priest was coming to a close, or if there was a way forward for me in the life of the church. In asking these questions, I had to come to terms with who I really am: one who lifts up the holy and the broken life of the church. In my own questions ran the questions of the church—who we really are. My colleague voiced that stunning need that I believe to be at the heart of the questions and worries before the institutional church: "Please, don't give us another hypothetical vision of what the church could be."

This next part starts with a searching response to that need. This is not another hypothetical vision of what the church could, should, might be. This is not the church as it wishes it were or as it struggles to be different. This is the sigh of resignation, where who we are finally catches up with us. This is the church as my sixteen-year-old self, realizing that I can't devote any more time to the version of myself that I wish I could be, when who I actually am is becoming so unavoidably clear. Even more importantly, this is the church where it is really alive, not the false version of church to which we inadvertently end up devoting so much energy. The thing that has to be named at the outset is that so much of the fear and the church's response to that fear, is tied up in propping up something that isn't real or true.

The institution of the church—the hierarchies, the voting mechanisms, the delineations of power, and the program departments—these can certainly serve a good and holy purpose. The structures of the church are dying, declining, being dismantled and called into question, and this has created enormous anxiety. But the structures and the institution are not the thing itself; it's not the alive, living thing that we call the body of Christ. The body of Christ is always the real, complicated, messy communities of people who have found themselves gathered together and who have been met by the surprising power of God's love.

The body of Christ is alive. It's not in decline. We don't have to manage it fearfully or try to make it something else or wish it were different. We do need to get better at seeing it and putting our energy and attention and time and love here. Ultrarealism isn't about giving up. It's about making sure that we're tuned in to the living, breathing truth. I suspect that starting with the truth, the church gathered—who we are and what that can mean—will be transformational in ways that surprise and bless us.

DISCUSSION QUESTIONS

1. Have you ever found your plans being interrupted by the sense that God was calling you elsewhere?

2. Here is the definition Martha offers of the church: "The Body of Christ is always the real, complicated, messy communities of people who have found themselves gathered together and who have been met by the surprising power of God's love." How do you connect with this definition? How would you define the church?

CHAPTER 7

The Church Is a Bad Mother

I Wanted This Book to Be One Thing, and This Is What I Got Instead

This book started with a conversation on an Easter Sunday night with my son, Gordon, who was then just about to turn ten. He was upset and crying. After much cajoling, he finally admitted to me the problem. He was in a full-fledged faith crisis.

"I d-d-d-don't th-th-think that I b-b-b-believe in . . ." he choked and cried and couldn't quite say the rest. After several loud gulping sobs, he finally spit it out. ". . . Jesus." He sounded as if his heart was breaking.

He had been asking me questions for months. "How do we know we can trust the Bible?" he wanted to know. "How about the dinosaurs? Why does it say that the world was created in seven days? I don't understand why Jesus is God. Does that mean that God wasn't in heaven for those years that Jesus was on earth? Why did Jesus have to suffer?" And in response to every meaningless tragedy, difficult death in the parish, and a whole variety of other sadnesses that we face, Gordon wanted to know the age-old question: "Why do these bad things have to happen?"

On that Easter night, I could do little other than hold him close, my hand resting on his chest, willing his breathing to settle and his heart to stop racing.

"At your baptism, we prayed for you to have an inquiring and discerning heart. That's what you have. That prayer is coming true. It's okay for you to have doubts and questions. God loves you. I love you. You don't need to be upset."

As a mother, I feel best when I can make things right for my kids, when I can bandage a scrape, talk them through a rough patch with friends, help them to find the courage to do difficult things, walk them through a math problem, feed them delicious homemade food that both gives them energy and communicates my love. I held Gordon and soothed him in that moment, but then I went into problem-solving mode. I wanted to bandage up and cobble together Gordon's faith for him too. I wanted to lead him from unbelief back to a truer and more fervent faith.

I went to my favorite defaults when trying to make sense of the world: I made a plan for my reading and writing. I pulled out some of C. S. Lewis' offerings from my bookshelf and ordered a few of the current best-sellers in Christian apologetics. I reminded myself that thinking people across the world and throughout time have also asked these very same things. I was reassured in knowing that great Christian thinkers have already teased out the rational and philosophical reasons for believing.

I began writing this book. I knew that Gordon's questions and struggle have a wider resonance. I saw a connection between his struggle and our mainline church's decline. I imagined not just equipping myself properly for responding to Gordon, but while I was at it, writing a chapter-by-chapter walk-through of easy, rational responses to the faith questions that felt most urgent and foundational.

"I'm writing a book on Christian apologetics," I told my brother, Andrew, while we were out for a sibling walk.

"That's a weird word for it," he responded. "It makes it sound as if you are sorry about believing." I explained to him that while the word apologetics does come from the Greek word for apology, it is used in its more ancient sense: to make a reasoned defense of something or someone. "It's about building the case," I concluded.

I wanted this book to be a smooth-talking and compelling case for faith. I wanted this book to tie up the church's decline in a nice, neat response, topped with a bow, and delivered as the ultimate gift of faith—to Gordon, to our congregations, and to the world.

The thing about gifts is we don't get to choose what they are. They are given to us. No consultation. I'm good at rational thought, careful research, and preparing properly for the tasks I need to do. But as I began to write about my faith, and more importantly our faith, it became clear that this gift had not come to me by way of my diligent and hardworking ways. It came to me through community and story. It also became obvious that in terms of any gifts I might have in sharing our faith with others, constructing a well-reasoned and meticulously prepared argument wasn't going to be my particular offering.

The problem with this realization is that what I do in fact have to offer starts with people and experiences that are not in any way able to be prettily packaged up with a nice, neat bow on top. My faith comes by way of the church—and that church can often look more like a liability than an asset.

The Kingdom Is Happening Now, Not Later

Jesus was an ultrarealist.

This can be seen most clearly in his arrival into public ministry, and in contrasting Jesus with his controversial, and also dangerous, mentor John the Baptist. John's message was typical in many ways to the prophetic tradition of which he was part. He called his people to repentance, to turn their lives back to God, and to be baptized as a public and sacramental sign of that turning.

The between-the-lines implication people read into John's message was if the people of Israel were to get their wayward lives back onto the right path, the kingdom of God would finally come among them, the evil occupying Romans could be vanquished, and a return to a self-governing, God-led model of political organization could be achieved.

When John was martyred and Jesus's public ministry began, the same political hope was placed on Jesus: maybe he would be the one to turn the tables, to overthrow Rome, and to reestablish God's rule here on earth among this particular people.

Jesus arrived, instead delivering a puzzling ultrareal message: "The Kingdom of God has drawn near!"

We can imagine the reaction to his proclamation might have been, "Where?" When Jesus arrived, nothing seemed categorically different. Rome was still very much in charge. Herod was still a far cry from any sort of King David. The people were still hungry and disenfranchised. The world was still a lousy mess, and none of what the people of Israel hoped for in their Messiah was seemingly on offer.

And yet, it's a proclamation that sets Jesus and his message distinctly apart: You don't have to wait; it's already happening. The rule of God, the power of God, the love of God is already on offer, is already being revealed. When Jesus said, "Repent," he was not calling people to get their lives back on track, he was inviting people to look again. Turn around; God is here!

The next thing Jesus did was call together a community. They weren't the brightest and best. Jesus didn't go trolling the halls of power; he didn't head hunt the most promising students of other rabbis. Instead, he assembled together a motley assortment of people who had crossed his path, whom he felt called to seek and meet. They were people whose need was evident, who had not been welcomed elsewhere, and some whose very presence was a source of controversy.

This is the ultrareal starting point of Jesus: the kingdom of God is right here, right now, in this disappointing mess of people.

The Case Hasn't Been Thrown Out of Court

This isn't a starting point that inspires easy belief. From those first disciples down to us today, and all of the screw-ups and failures in between, it feels like the church could be much better served by just editing out all of the bad witnesses who have done a crappy job of attending to the nearness of the kingdom of God.

And at the same time, what may be the most compelling reason to believe that Jesus was on to something is the fact that people still love, serve, and belong to the church even though time and time again it has done such a blisteringly bad job of revealing anything other than its own brokenness.

Somehow or other, faith still happens.

The church community in which I serve is peppered with men and women of a certain age who got divorced from marriages that weren't working and who were told by their church that they couldn't be remarried in the eyes of their Christian faith. They were told that their new marriage constituted adultery according to one decontextualized word of Jesus—who was arguably speaking against men leaving their wives destitute in a cultural landscape where widowed, unmarried, or divorced women were especially vulnerable because they only had status and protection through the men in their lives.

There are the heartbreaking experiences of the LGBTQ2+ Christian community, whose relationships were so long forced into the closet, were invalidated, slandered, condemned, and demonized because they didn't conform to the heterosexual norm. My friend and deacon of our church, Lorenzo, refers to the "clobber passages" of scripture—those seven instances where scripture speaks against sexual activity between people of the same gender. The fact that these passages are not referring to consensual, committed, loving, same-gender sex, or any sort of understanding of how people might be biologically geared toward same-gender attraction, is not taken into account; these passages have been used by the church to clobber people with the wrongness of their love.

In the years that I have been part of national gatherings of our Canadian Anglican Church, I have witnessed a number of specific and emotional apologies from the church to Indigenous people for the ways in which their beliefs and language were condemned by the Church who named them as "primitive" and "heathen," not to mention the Church's role in forcibly taking Indigenous children from their homes and families and putting them into schools that we now know were abusive and deadly in so many horrific ways. We know that much of this horror was intentional, that there was a whole system codified into law and enacted in specific ways to eradicate Indigenous people among us. We know that the Church blindly, willingly, enthusiastically even, participated in this eradication. We know this story of the colonizing church and its inherent racism is a common one across the globe.

What is amazing in these apologies is that people who were at the receiving end of the abuse are not only still willing to be part of our Church, but that they have become strong and true leaders within it. It is similarly amazing that we would still have LGBTQ2+ people in our churches or that we still have remarried divorced people in our churches—even after essential relationships of their lives, essential aspects of their own selves, were so relentlessly named as sinful and unwelcome. It is amazing that anybody chooses not just to continue in the life of the church, but that they can still hear the gospel.

Lorenzo was subjected to decades of trauma-inducing conversion therapy as he struggled to keep up the appearance of being a heterosexual male leader in the Churches of Christ denomination in which he served. This "therapy" did incalculable damage to his psyche. And yet, through it all, he never lost sight of his love for God—or most especially, God's love for him. When he finally came out of the closet and left that denomination, he didn't leave the church. Instead, he found his way to the Anglican Church and became a deacon devoted to seeking out the disenfranchised and speaking to them and offering them concrete acts of care and compassion that reveal God's love for them.

Many who have been abused by the church have needed to walk away. Their reasons are understandable. But the ones who have chosen to stay offer an enormously powerful witness. The church is a different community, a community that has received great blessing, because the voices of those who have been disenfranchised have stuck around persistently enough to speak a different truth, to call us all to hear afresh a gospel that we have been so bad at living out, to invite and invite and invite us all again to see and hear and receive the blessing of voices we thought needed to be corrected, hidden, dismissed, or made to conform.

"The Church is a bad mother," my friend and mentor Michael used to quip when I ran up against the comparatively minor frustrations and hurts that the church would deal my way. It's a funny statement that reveals our community as the flawed entity it is—not an especially beautiful bride of Christ, or a warm and nurturing place in which faith can flourish, but one riddled by carelessness, thoughtlessness, and even abuse.

The Ballot and the Bread

I can't say that I have experienced the abuse of the church, but I have been hurt. I have run up against entrenched biases and even misogyny against female leadership. I have received stinging critiques about everything from the cut of my hair, to the length of my skirt, to the beliefs that I try to express. I have been leered at by parishioners and by colleagues. Like many women, in the church or not, my body and my looks get treated like public property and are considered to be a reasonable topic of discussion in everything from a colleague's sermon to the area-wide gatherings of our clergy.

A few years ago I was on the ballot in our diocese as they elected a new bishop. After the voting was over, I was on the receiving end of a wonderful outcome. I didn't get elected. I got to continue serving in ministry in an incredibly fruitful community of faith. And the Diocese of Niagara got a smart, capable, imaginative, and energetic new bishop. Nonetheless, I walked away from the election feeling like I had been crushed underneath a toppled skyscraper.

I had been strong-armed into being on that ballot with pleas, mostly from senior male clergy of the church, to provide an option for voting in the first female bishop of our diocese. Although it was clear that I was a token of something, I was also led to believe my being on that ballot was more than tokenism. I had served the Church in a wide range of leadership roles. I had proven myself as a collaborative and experienced and visionary leader.

It was with a lot of prayer and discernment—with my family, my spiritual director, and in conversation with some trusted friends—that I felt like it was the right thing to allow my name to stand. I don't regret that I said yes. It may have started with strong-arming, but it ended up feeling like the work of the Holy Spirit.

The Holy Spirit certainly had to work overtime because the experience gave me a shocking view of the Church's misogyny. Although it was the other woman on the ballot who was elected, and our Church did indeed get its first female bishop, the narrative to which I was subjected was eye-opening. Other candidates were asked about their ideas for the future of the Church, I was asked how I thought I was going to manage the job when I had young children at home. A male colleague flat out told me, in the presence of other fellow priests, that he thought that it was wrong for me even to consider the job because of my children. He assumed that my being bishop would mean that they would no longer be my top priority. Other candidates received commentary on the words that they shared; I received commentary on my shoes.

"At least we got the right gender," one of those senior male colleagues who had encouraged me to be on the ballot commented to me in the hallway after the election. This was demeaning to both me and our newly elected bishop, but this male priest said it in an offhand manner, and I didn't have the wherewithal to call him out on it.

Afterward, I wanted to burn every bridge I could find. At first this instinct was about anger. As the anger calmed down, it was about protecting myself, to get some of my insides out of the way of direct exposure. I wanted to swear off the Church and my leadership in it and sever the relationships I perceived as having betrayed me.

Like every person on the ballot, I had to lead worship the day after the electoral synod. I would have paid a queen's ransom to have stayed home instead. I did not want to have to speak about the results of the previous day. I did not want to face even one member of the body of Christ. There are not many places on earth that I could have gone that morning and received such an outpouring of faithfulness and love other than St. George's, St. Catharines, and as grateful as I was for them, it was desperately hard to open my heart back up to receive anything resembling the kindness and care of the Church.

Something happened that morning, though, something that gets at the truth of who we really are and how the gift of faith really works, even with the meanness, misogyny, and bad witnesses. I shared in the praise and prayer of our faith community, almost viscerally squirming at having to be there. Our bishop-in-residence, retired bishop of Niagara, Walter, had been slated to preach that morning. As always, he spoke beautifully and eloquently. What's more, he spoke right to me. He publicly affirmed and celebrated me and my ministry. I cried from the beginning to the end.

As meaningful as that was, his words weren't what confronted my bitter heart with the truth and healing I had not wanted. When I gave out the broken bread to the church, my innermost thoughts were laid bare before God—every egotistical tendency and shattered dream. And somehow, I unwittingly caught a glimpse of not me, but us, us as we really are: perfect and beloved and beautiful and fed.

We are people who God chooses to walk alongside through the person of Jesus. I could see again his heart was fragile, and yet in him we see God's purpose not just for him, but for every person. I could see how God was even then in that moment gathering up the broken and fragmented pieces of our lives in order to see through the life, death, and resurrection of Jesus a wholeness in us that we can't see ourselves.

We are not merely a collection of our missteps and disappointments and crashing failures. We are also the body of Christ. Jesus keeps showing up in us, especially in those moments when we are hurting, Jesus shows up for us. Our witness isn't always good. Sometimes it is downright awful. Jesus still shows up and is at work in us. And in that visceral reality is a gritty, not pretty, response to why we might continue to gather in prayer and say "I believe," no matter the unwanted circumstances, not to mention the people with whom we would rather not have to walk.

This doesn't make for easy answers, and it's not easy to tie up with a bow. But for so many of us, it's the only reason in the end that the case hasn't been thrown out of court.

DISCUSSION QUESTIONS

1. Do you relate to Gordon's faith struggle and questions? How has the church around you responded when you have had doubts or questions?

2. Have you ever struggled in your faith because of how you see the church behaving? What has kept you in the church in times like those?

3. How much do you think about how your own behavior bears witness to the truth of the things we believe?

4. Jesus's message is that the kingdom of God has already drawn near. God isn't waiting until we're better behaved or more faithful to be at work in us. Where do you experience the truth "the Kingdom of God is among us"?

CHAPTER 8

Why I Didn't Start My Own Church

Which One Is True?

One Christmas Eve, Cheryl grabbed me as we were setting up for our second service of the night. She wanted to introduce me to Danah, who was sitting in one of the front pews and was wearing the traditional head covering of a Muslim woman. She looked to be in her early twenties. I was grateful that Danah had connected with Cheryl, one of the warmest and friendliest people on the planet. I went over to introduce myself and to say how glad we were that she was with us.

Danah made a point of being outgoing, and she quickly became part of a circle of friendship in the church. I learned later, though, that there were things that surprised her about St. George's. She was surprised by being welcomed (she had not been welcomed in other churches she had tried out); she was surprised at the openness of our preaching; and most of all, she was surprised that she could ask questions.

And she asked a lot of questions. Danah was studying science, with the goal of eventually going to med school, and she brought her brilliant scientific mind to religion. Danah asked me detailed questions by email and in conversation about why I did or did not say one thing or another in my sermons, what the church did or did not believe about God and Jesus. She particularly wanted to know which religion—Islam or Christianity—is true. Danah didn't realize that as she fired her questions at me, she was hooking in me a long-standing source of internal conflict about my own Christian faith.

Why I Didn't Start My Own Church

When I finished my undergrad degree in music, I didn't see myself as part of the church any longer. My adoration of Jesus remained strong, but I wasn't sure I wanted to be included in the label "Christian" because the church had gotten so many things wrong about Jesus and about its witness in the world. I was particularly troubled by any baked-in exclusivity that Christianity promoted. I had taken classes in world religions and philosophy of religion, and I saw great beauty and dignity in other religious faiths. I felt sure that Jesus would not have appreciated the high horse onto which Christians have all too often climbed in supposing ourselves to have ownership of the truth. I hated that wars have been waged against other faiths. I was disgusted by the Crusades and the Inquisition. I saw Christianity as bankrupt and believed that other faith traditions were much more interesting, perhaps even more pure. I wanted to learn about Buddhism and Islam and Baha'i.

I was also mostly untethered from an actual relationship with the church. Even though I continued to show up on Sunday mornings to sing in the cathedral choir, I didn't show up ready to listen. I assumed that I was more evolved than anything that might be offered from the pulpit, and I sat through the services with that attitude. In my mind, being part of the community of the choir didn't exactly feel like being part of the church.

I want to be clear that these various feelings and assumptions were purely my own and not representative of how faithfully and compellingly the people in that church were living their lives. I had gotten myself cut off from receiving the faith that was no doubt on offer all around me.

The funny thing is that when I finished my music degree, I still felt called to become a priest. This sense was nothing other than a gut instinct, because certainly my idea of what I would do as a priest was wildly unrealistic. I saw my version of priestly ministry being somewhat akin to the work of a career counselor or travel agent. I thought that people would come to me with their religious needs and questions and, based on a kind of spiritual personality inventory, I would line them up with a faith offering that would best suit and serve them. I imagined that I could prepare immersive experiences for a congregation that might be more interested in a potpourri of faith rather than settling on just one version of religion. It seemed like a solution to what I saw as Christianity's central problem: we're just too full of ourselves.

Yes, Jesus says that he is the way, the truth, and the life. He says in the same breath that nobody comes to the Father except through him. But he is also clear that his followers are not to punch above their weight in thinking that they are in charge of judging the soul of another person, particularly in terms of whether that soul is close to God. Jesus had little patience for anyone assuming their religious labels gives them a superior position in God's eyes. He reserved his harshest words for those who relied on their religious identity to assure themselves of God's favor toward them, particularly when that arrogance becomes coupled with pointing one's fingers at those who supposedly don't make the cut.

Jesus embraced in his own meal ministry a symmetry with the eternal banquet depicted by the prophet Isaiah, telling us of a God who never gives up on calling all people to set aside their differences, to come and find their seat at the table:

> On this mountain the Lord of hosts will make for
>   all people
> a feast of rich food, a feast of well-aged wines,
> of rich food filled with marrow, of well-aged
>   wines strained clear. (Isa. 25:6)

I suspect that the humble and boundary-breaking reign of God, seen in Jesus, actually calls us to affirm God's salvific love as clearly, compellingly, and powerfully at work in those who don't explicitly claim to follow Jesus's way. That is to say: following the way of Jesus compels us to name the way of Jesus in those who don't think they follow the way of Jesus. It was this picture of Jesus that was leading me into ministry. I wanted to create a church that would be truer to what I thought this radical Savior was all about.

I was in good company. Countless people have looked at the complicated landscape that is the church and wanted to create something a whole lot simpler, truer, and more straightforward. From the people and places described on the pages of scripture to today, that impulse has been continually present, and it has resulted in the creation of more versions of church, more denominations, than can be counted.

The amazing thing in this impulse is how thoroughly unsuccessful it has ever been in making things simpler. Wherever you go, whatever version of the "true faith" you seek to live, the inescapable fact is that there is a whole world of others out there believing that they are living the true faith too.

I didn't consider any of these inescapable facts when I made my way to seminary with my head full of dreams for how I would correct the church. I didn't consider the irony of how my desire to create a new and better church might actually be buying into exactly the mistake that I thought I hated about the church. I wanted to correct the arrogance of the church's thinking we have the right answer. I also thought *I* had the right answer, which is exactly what has been such a source of division in the church: the idea that I know something about Jesus that everyone else has overlooked; the idea that a new church based on this overlooked truth is the solution.

Live for Good

My spiritual director, Kevin, also found himself at a crossroads in his early twenties. He was raised in the Mennonite tradition, called to be a pastor like his dad before him, but he dropped out of seminary after one year. His faith was in shambles. He wasn't sure if he believed in God anymore. He decided to become a carpenter. (Maybe he didn't want to be too far from Jesus, even in this faith crisis.)

Kevin is a voracious reader, and at the time he was reading Tolstoy's *Anna Karenina*. He said it was the single most influential and important book in his life. He loaned me his copy. It was obvious from the missing cover and the book spine that has long since snapped in two, the dog-eared pages and his name written in pen on the inside first page, it was a book that he has read so many times that it had literally fallen apart.

It takes the lead character over 900 pages to come to the central insight of the book. The main character, Levin, had wrestled with his faith. He wondered both at his friends who didn't believe and didn't seem troubled in the least by the lack of God in their lives, as well as the realization that the people he truly admired were believers. It was in his interactions with a peasant man named Theodore that suddenly he understood a basic truth with burning clarity. Theodore noted that there are certain people who "live for their bellies," which of course is an understandable biological impulse. It's the impulse for self-preservation and survival. But there are also those who live for truth, who live for God. This other way of living could be further simplified and clarified. We should live for what is good. That's it. Our lives should serve goodness. Levin believed that this insight is something that we can all agree on. He says, "I had been seeking miracles; I regretted not having seen a miracle that would have convinced me. And here is a miracle, the only possible one, everlasting, surrounding me on all sides—and I never noticed it!"[1]

Kevin described being similarly thunderstruck by this simple revelation. He said that he was still agnostic about many things, including God's existence, but he accepted that there was a basic choice that we face. We can serve ourselves, or we can serve what is good. This insight allowed Kevin to return to the Christian faith. He came back not sure of any of the dogmatic things that get said about Jesus, but he accepted that if we want to know what serving good looks like, serving something other than just ourselves, then Jesus gives us a model. Kevin wanted to follow this model, not the one that pursues just the "filling of our own bellies."

---

1   Leo Tolstoy, *Anna Karenina* (New York: New American Library, 1961), 915.

Unlike Kevin, I went into seminary with my faith already in shambles. Within days of starting my classes, something happened that I didn't anticipate. I picked up my assigned books from Crux bookstore across the street from Trinity College and began learning from bright, compassionate, open-minded, and thoughtful teachers about the inexhaustible beauty of our own faith. I attended daily chapel and heard our prayers and hymns in a new way, as I also heard a different person each day invite us into an exploration of the day's texts. I was humbled in the most exciting and enlivening way as I fell headlong into this glorious revelation: there was actually no chance of me, or anyone else for that matter, ever having ownership of the truth.

At our best, Christianity doesn't claim a position of arrogance but one of open-hearted searching. We don't have the right answers; we have this astonishing permission to keep exploring all of the questions. And we have a promise that Jesus is with us, hand in hand, in that exploration.

At baptisms in our faith tradition, we pray that the newly baptized will have "inquiring and discerning hearts" with "the courage to will and to persevere" in their knowledge and love of God. The faith of Jesus equips our inquiry and our discernment. I didn't need to correct the church into offering a potpourri of faith options. I just needed to be the kind of leader who invites others to keep plumbing the inexhaustible riches of what this faith tradition offers.

Both/And

There is an implicit corrective that allowed both Kevin and me to continue in the faith, eventually becoming Christian leaders. It comes from the realm of mental health—which leads me to my friend Caitlyn.

Caitlyn has borderline personality disorder (BPD), which is a serious diagnosis, and Caitlyn is careful not to glamorize it. People with BPD can struggle to maintain relationships and can engage in self-harm and addictive or impulsive behaviors, and they are at risk of dying by suicide at a much higher than normal rate. At the heart of the presenting behaviors is an unstable or shifting sense of self.

The main treatment for BPD is dialectical behavior therapy (DBT). While the description of DBT sounds to me like healthy life skills that could benefit anyone, Caitlyn reminds me that this therapy can be the difference between life and death for someone with BPD. DBT is not unlike ultrarealism. In running, we use ultrarealism to comprehensively identify the state of affairs we are actually encountering in the moment—not what we wish were different or what we worry might happen—and then basing our decisions and running actions on the circumstances before us. DBT and ultrarealism are both an intentional embrace of acceptance and change.

In DBT, Caitlyn talks about learning the importance of the words both/and. Caitlyn is beautiful and beloved in the core of her being, and there are things that she needs to change. These things are both true. Caitlyn can feel pain in navigating the world because of the intensity of her emotions. She needs a tool kit of strategies to use in seeking to even out the emotional rollercoaster that is her life, to be able to breathe, to pause before reacting and temper that pain with something other than self-destructive numbing behaviors. And at the same time, Caitlyn brings a fierce and insightful creativity to everything that she does because of her intense emotions. These are both true too. The suffering is real and so is the offering.

I am convinced that this kind of both/and thinking is exactly what allowed the Christian church to thrive and expand in the first place. Paul, the great evangelist of the Roman Empire, was someone who intuitively understood the principles of DBT. His burning insight when he was first proclaiming Jesus across the Roman Empire started with an either/or attitude, but it was in his both/and embrace where he connected. He visited Athens, where he was "distressed" by the idols to all of the different gods across the city. And yet, here is how he talked to the Athenians:

Athenians, I see how extremely religious you are in every way. For as I went through the city and looked carefully at the objects of your worship, I found among them an altar with the inscription, "To an unknown god." What therefore you worship as unknown, this I proclaim to you. . . . From one ancestor he made all nations to inhabit the whole earth . . . so that they would search for God and perhaps grope for him and find him—though indeed he is not far from each one of us. (Acts 17:22–24, 26–27)

I love this passage. The truth that it names is clear and bright and bold. No matter who we are or what culture or religion we are from, we are built with the desire to "search for God and perhaps grope for him and find him." And lo and behold, God is not far from each one of us.

Paul taught the Athenians, who were thirsty for knowledge and for wisdom. He taught them based on what they already knew. He spoke to their religious hearts, their ingrained religious instinct. He didn't tell them that they were wrong. He offered them a next step on their quest for truth. They had access to truth, to God and God's love. And also, there is an offering of God's love in Jesus that is life-giving and generous and that is for them too. These things are both true. God is not far from any one of us. And the way of salvation is opened to us in Jesus. These things are both true too.

The Ultrareal Church Is Both/And

I don't know why God doesn't work in a more direct and clear manner. I don't know why there are such divergent understandings of God, especially when so many wars have been fought and so many lives lost in the name of one version over and against other versions. This plays out on the very grand stage of differing world religions, but it also plays out within our own Christian faith, even within our own separate denominations. It can be confusing to consider how my fellow human beings come to articulate their experience of God, and what God is up to, in ways that I find so at odds with what I believe.

Confusion is one word. Anger, disappointment, and judgment are other words. Who among us in the life of faith hasn't felt at one time or another that this whole faith thing would work a lot better if we could just categorically edit out those who see things in ways that I don't understand, accept, or agree with? That desire to either bolt and start our own church or eject out of the church those who don't pass muster is written like angry red welts all across our Christian history, not to mention all across the history of religious warfare.

The violence might not answer any questions for me. It might not help me better accept or explain why God can't just speak much more directly into our human lives. But that violence, the wars and bloodshed, the broken relationships and the division across our human family, points to why it is so important to embrace what we know rather than rail against what we don't understand or what we wish could be different.

We know that God loves us. Therefore, we also know that God doesn't set us up with random tests in order to see if we pass or fail. God hasn't allowed various world religions to flourish in order to fill out a divine scorecard based on whether we answered the question of religion correctly.

If this is true, once again we are stuck with one another. We're stuck with the confusion of different viewpoints and stories and experiences. Our lives are bound up in one another, whether we like it or not. God has very clearly chosen—for reasons I don't always comprehend—to speak in and through our difference *and* our connectedness. God is at work in the ways that we don't agree and when our viewpoints feel a million miles away from one another. God is at work in the truth of how biologically and spiritually we are interconnected; God is at work in the truth that our relationship with one another is actually nonnegotiable.

The ultrareal church is the church of both/and.

Danah's Email

I couldn't give Danah the straightforward answer she wanted. She was frustrated with me, and I was frustrated with myself after some of our conversations. She hooked in me the central discomfort I have felt with Christianity's implicit arrogance. But she also hooked in me that basic desire to be the sort of person, the sort of leader, who has an arsenal of straightforward and clear answers to Danah's kind of questions. When Danah asked me one simple question—"Which one is true?"—I stumbled over my answer. "Which one is true?" is not a question I know how to answer.

There is an idea about religion that has had a lot of currency in the last number of years, which is that it's the churches with the straightforward answers to the questions of faith that hold the greatest mass appeal. This may have statistical merit. What is definitely true though is that there has to be room for those of us who need the both/and of faith.

Although I could not provide Danah with the definitive answer that she was seeking, she seemed both frustrated and compelled by my lack of clarity. In one breath, she sighed with exasperation that I couldn't just tell her that Christianity was right and Islam wrong. And in the next breath, she admitted that if it were up to her and would not wreak havoc on her family life, she would like to be Christian. A few days after our conversation, she sent me this email:

> I learned that even if I was not born as a Christian, Jesus Christ still loves me and talks with me.
>
> I learned that some drawbacks in life give us a greater thrust forward. When I went to Jesus Christ with broken wings, he sent me back FLYING. At that same time, Jesus promised me: "I have come into the world as light, so that whoever believes in me may not remain in darkness.
>
> When I first joined [St. George's], I was surprised that my fellow Christians were talking about the same God that I'm thinking about. Thus, I learned that he is the same God, but each one of us has their own way in believing in him.

I am searching for the truth. I learned that I have just dipped myself into a deep ocean. Whenever I learn something new, I realize that there is a whole world out there that I still don't know about.

DISCUSSION QUESTIONS

1. Martha asks, "Who among us in the life of faith hasn't felt at one time or another that this whole faith thing would work a lot better if we could just categorically edit out those who see things in ways that I don't understand, accept, or agree with?" Do you relate to this statement? How do you deal with knowing that your fellow Christians understand the faith so differently from you?

2. How do you connect with the idea that our faith gives us companionship and permission in exploring life's questions rather than an arsenal of all of the right answers?

3. Where have you experienced beauty, truth, and connection in other faith traditions? Where have you felt compelled or enriched by beliefs other than our own?

CHAPTER 9

The Flaws Are Kind of the Point

Bob on the Dock with Jesus

Bob Donald could give you the impression that he was laidback, that he didn't get too fussed about details—what people thought, appearances, or the little day-to-day worries that weigh the rest of us down. He cried openly and often; he sang and laughed loudly; he didn't mind being wrong or repeating himself. His heart was unnervingly unguarded. One of my favorite images of Bob was from a story he told me when I was training for my first half-marathon.

"I ran a half-marathon once," he said, smiling widely. "The little truck that gathers up the pylons at the end followed me all the way to the finish line. But I did it!" Bob was proud in the best sense of the word. He was able to own his accomplishments without false modesty and with a sort of luminous joy. He was a big man—tall and heavy, and his footfall could best be described as "lumbering." "A big teddy bear" is how he often got styled, but in no way did he move as someone full of fluff. He walked with weight.

Although I never saw him cross that half-marathon finish line, I can see him clearly in my mind's eye. I can see his slow, plodding, slightly awkward but persistent and joyful steps bringing up the rear of the race. I can see him not getting the least bit flustered by the person in the truck gathering up the pylons, because Bob was not embarrassed to be last; he was proud to keep going. I know he would have won over the guy in the truck and anyone else who was left at the finish line. They would have all been rooting for Bob to finish the race. Bob is the image I see when I hear that popular verse from the letter to the Hebrews:

> Therefore, since we are surrounded by so great a cloud of witnesses, let us also lay aside every weight and the sin that clings so closely, and let us run with perseverance the race that is set before us, looking to Jesus the pioneer and perfecter of our faith, who for the sake of the joy that was set before him endured the cross, disregarding its shame, and has taken his seat at the right hand of the throne of God. (Heb. 12:1–2)

It's as though the author of that letter knew Bob—this big, lumbering man, who was heavy and weightless in all the best ways, who kept putting one foot diligently in front of the other, and all for the sake of joy.

You could be forgiven for thinking that Bob was laidback, and in some ways he was. Early into my time at St. David Anglican-Lutheran Church in Orillia, a man came by to talk about our church potentially putting on a dinner for the group he led. When he met me, he made a mildly lewd comment about my looks, to which I responded as I usually do, with an embarrassed and uncertain half-laugh. Bob looked murderously at the man and wrapped up the meeting without securing a firm plan for the dinner. "What a jerk," he said to me after he left. The dinner never happened.

As a female leader, people routinely assume I am fair game for endless comments about my appearance. Bob was horrified on my behalf in a way that was surprising because of how rarely anyone reacts to those kind of comments as anything other than the cost of doing business. Bob was laidback—except when he wasn't.

Bob had the ability to singe you with the intensity of his focus. He wasn't intense about being at the front of the pack. He wasn't intense about appearances or what people thought of him. He was intense about his love for Jesus, and that love was entirely, completely, and fully wrapped up in his love for the church. He was a family man, for sure, beloved by his wife, children, and grandchildren. Somehow he also managed to take seriously Jesus's call to widen our scope on who family actually is. His family was never limited to his blood relatives. His family was all of us in the church, all served by the church, all who might be his neighbors, all who had the privilege of crossing his path. He loved us all in a way that let us know we were his family.

For these reasons, Bob was the consummate evangelist. We had adult baptisms fairly regularly at St. David, and almost to a person, Bob was the one that people asked to stand up with them as their sponsor, or, as he liked to joke, "The Godfather." He made loving Jesus seem approachable, reasonable, and joyful. He made loving Jesus feel like something really good—like the warm, fresh-out-of-the-oven flatbread he would bring with him every Saturday for our afternoon Fam Jam worship service. Loving Jesus was delicious and wonderful, not something that required forcing anything down someone's throat.

The other image that comes to mind is the one that Bob shared in a book study that we led one Easter. It was the year that the book *The Shack* blew up. Our congregation wanted to read it, so we offered a four-week post-Easter study to discuss it. It is the story of Mack, a man whose young daughter is tragically kidnapped and murdered, which propels him into questioning his faith. In a visit to the shack where Mack's daughter Missy had been held captive before her death, Mack is visited by God. God shows up in three different ways—as a nurturing and maternal Black woman (the Parent), as a carpenter (the Son), and as a semitransparent spirit figure (the Holy Spirit). At one point, Mack lies on the dock with the carpenter Jesus, under a vast starry sky, and receives the fullness of God's friendship, companionship, and faithfulness. It is a healing moment for Mack.

It became Bob's signature image of God. He referenced it not only in that study, but in other studies, meetings, and faith reflections that we shared over the years. God was the dear, faithful friend who will lie under a starry sky with you in the middle of nowhere and talk with you through the night.

The author of Hebrews wrote we "look to Jesus as the pioneer and perfecter of our faith." Bob ran that race with persistent, slow, plodding steps, not caring where in the pack he ended up. As he did, he looked to Jesus. His love for the church, for his neighbors, for his family—in the widest sense of what that means—was entirely centered in his love for Jesus.

Not Perfect

My recounting of Bob's witness sounds a bit like hagiography, the type of Christian literature that remembers the saints as superhuman superheroes of the faith, glossing over any flaws and exaggerating the good deeds and extraordinary happenings in order to paint some sort of picture of how belief in Jesus and personal goodness go together. But anyone who knew Bob will tell you that he was far from perfect. He could easily be blinded by his love for the church. He led too much with his heart and got into hot water by letting things like protocol, procedure, and collaboration fall by the wayside. He put his foot in his mouth a little more frequently than most people I know. When he realized he had misspoken, his face turned a bright tomato red. It's very important to say that he wasn't perfect, because that is part of Bob's witness too. He loved and served Jesus in imperfect ways. That's kind of the point.

We Don't Love in the Abstract.
The Flaws Are Kind of the Point.

In J. M. Coetzee's book *Slow Man*, the character Paul is a bachelor who falls in love with the nurse who cares for him as he recovers from a bicycle accident. He not only falls in love with her, he falls in love with her children as he searches for meaning in his life. He opens his home to her wayward teenaged son Drago, whom he quickly finds to be messy and disruptive. Drago takes advantage of his generosity with a surprising lack of gratitude. A wise woman in Paul's life, Elizabeth Costello, counsels him:

> In the abstract I am sure you would like to love young Drago, but the facts of life keep getting in the way. We cannot love by an act of will, Paul. We have to learn. That is why souls descend from their realm on high and

consent to being born again; so that, as they grow up in our company, they can lead us along the hard road of loving.[1]

We don't get to love in the abstract. We only love in the particular. And we are only loved in the particular. As Coetzee so brilliantly frames it, this is the "hard road of loving." It's no Hallmark card.

Jesus promises that "where two or three are gathered together, I am in your midst." Jesus makes very few, if any, promises to just the individual person. Even the Lord's Prayer is prayed as a collective: Our Father, give us our daily bread, forgive us as we forgive others. Dear Lord, save us. While Jesus was still in the thick of his own ministry, he was already setting up the community through which his life and presence would continue beyond his own flesh-and-blood existence. The church is not styled as a building, not as a collection of friends or even of like-minded people, but as a body: the body of Christ. None of us has any real choice about finding ourselves attached to one another: the eyes and ears, the stomach and bowel, the toenails and saliva and ear wax are all necessary for the function of the whole. None of the parts gets the offering of an opt-out. Apart from one another, the individual parts cannot live.

But getting mixed up with the church is risky. That there is no real opt-out doesn't mean that opting out isn't incredibly appealing.

Our flaws are discussed in the same passage where Jesus says that he'll be present to us whenever we gather as a group. That promise is preceded by some pretty detailed directions about how we're to sort out our inevitable fights. It is followed by words on the ongoing need for forgiveness as we navigate our complex relationships.

Bob occasionally got himself and others into a real pickle. I say that not as a knock against Bob, but because he is representative of how even the best of the best can get things wrong.

---

1 J. M. Coetzee, *Slow Man* (London: Secker & Warburg, 2005), 182.

Depending on your experience with the church, you have probably known something, either personally or through the headlines, of how the church gets it wrong. You may have been hurt, even profoundly, by the church getting it wrong.

Most of us who served with Bob would legitimately list him among the saints. But the church is also filled with people who aren't just flawed, they are bad. There are deceitful, manipulative, power-hungry, and predatory people in the church too.

Among all of the risky things that Jesus did, leaving the continuation of his ministry up to us was the riskiest of them all. But there isn't any other way. As I said, the flaws are kind of the point. Jesus didn't just show up to reveal God to us. Jesus showed up to redeem us. In Jesus, God reaches out to each of us and all of us, to name and claim the truth of who we are for the purpose and plan of love. The Good News is that this love is offered and made possible in us, even though we aren't perfect. Here is the heart of grace: to be loved without deserving it. More importantly, it is the heart of grace for God to see the goodness, beauty, and possibility for love in us when we have lost sight of it ourselves.

For that reason, God chose that the life and work of Jesus would continue in the world through our bodies, through the flawed and sometimes downright sinful people that God is in the business of claiming as good, beautiful, loved, and loving.

I need the church in order to believe in Jesus because it's only through the community of faith that Jesus's promise to be present to us is most faithfully enacted. I need the church in order to believe in Jesus because that is the living, breathing witness to what Jesus is actually up to, other than just showing up. I need this mess of sin and blindness and fatal flaws in order to see for myself how grace really works, how love and forgiveness and redemption are real and powerful. Saying that Jesus is God is just an interesting thing to say, unless it has something to do with us. Not us as we wish we might be, or think we should be, but us as we really are.

DISCUSSION QUESTIONS

1. Consider a saint in your life. Who is someone who has inspired faith in you, who has brought you closer to God? What are their good qualities? Can you also see their flaws?

2. We need one another in order to know and love Jesus. We need one another's flaws, too, in order to be able to see how God is truly at work in our lives, even through our flaws. It is easy to become disillusioned with the church when we see her people behaving badly. We wish that faith could make people more obviously better. Why might it be helpful to be reminded that "the flaws are kind of the point"?

3. Jesus doesn't show up in our lives just as companion and friend, although companionship is no small thing. Jesus shows up to redeem us. To be drawn into relationship with God exactly as we are is to know healing and wholeness. Is this hard to accept? For ourselves or for others? That God could work in me, and in you, even when we're so far from perfect?

CHAPTER 10

Jesus Looks Like Dirty Feet

Dirty Feet

I see Jesus as a pair of dirty feet.

As I have written about extensively, I suffered from an eating disorder when I was younger. I had no sense that there was any way out of my illness. I expected to despise my body as long as it refused to conform to the standard of beauty I had been taught was the one and only marker of health and wellness. I expected to be at war with food and with my very own flesh until the day that I finally won that war, the diet worked, and the fat-free version of me was finally liberated for all the world to see.

But in one desperate night of prayer, I found myself asking for healing. Until that moment, I hadn't known I wanted healing or even that it could be possible apart from the possibility of dropping twenty pounds. After reading the Bible that night, I let my mind imagine the details of the story of a blind man named Bartimaeus crying out to Jesus along the roadside. When I tried to locate myself in the story, I was the one pleading for help. I saw Jesus's dirty, travel-worn feet in front of me. I desperately held his feet, not daring to look up. I couldn't see his face, not because it wasn't there, but because I couldn't bring myself to raise my eyes. I didn't want to stay locked in the unrelenting patterns of misery and guilt that I felt about everything that I ate. Even though I couldn't put words to what I was asking, I felt that Jesus heard and understood. I woke up several hours later to a violent stomach flu. It felt like something ugly was being expelled from my body.

For the most part, those who knew Jesus during his physical life seem to have been amazed by his healing, drawn in by his teaching, and put off by those moments when Jesus's relationship with God became too close for comfort. And yet, in the weeks, months, and years following those strange collective encounters with the risen Jesus, they felt their connection to Jesus actually growing. This is what came to be described as the movement of the Holy Spirit. Somehow the movement of the Holy Spirit allowed them to put language to an experience of Jesus that they had only begun to recognize while he was with them. As they knew the surprising and undeniable presence and love of Jesus, they also came to realize that they knew God. I have seen Jesus in Bob, in my parishioners and fellow Christians of all colors and backgrounds. I have seen how Jesus shows up and how people bear witness to the love and peace they receive when he does. I myself have been set free by the Lord who heard my prayer for a healing I didn't even know could be possible.

A Face We Do and Don't Recognize

I have never heard another person describe Jesus's overwhelming feature as being his dirty feet. The uniqueness of our experiences of Jesus is both a good thing and a source of frustration. You would think that Jesus, the embodied revelation of God, would pin God down, would let us know once and for all what God is actually like, what God looks like, even. That's part of the appeal, no doubt, of the Shroud of Turin, the supposed imprint of Jesus's face. The God who walked among us left us with visual artifacts. We get to see God with our own eyes too, just like the disciples who walked the dusty road with Jesus. There's nothing wrong with that impulse, except when it then leads any of us to think that we ourselves have the definitive picture of who God is.

Yes, Jesus is that hand reaching out to us. Jesus is that friend who walks alongside us. Jesus is the one who has a story of birth, suffering, death, friendship, and learning in which we can see and connect something of our own stories. Pinning God down into a person's story allows us to know and love God in a very powerful way.

Yet even in this flesh-and-blood person, we have to keep being surprised by the God who refuses to be owned by any of us.

Jesus shows up the way that Jesus shows up. All of those blond-haired, blue-eyed, white, white, white pictures of Jesus that hang in countless Sunday schools across North America, especially through the last century, say to the white people that Jesus looks like them. But we must remember that Jesus doesn't only look like them!

Gary, a member of our congregation and a feminist male of Indigenous descent, sees Jesus as a female and a mother. He is in the good company of mystics like Julian of Norwich, who wrote compellingly about her visions of Jesus as a loving mother.

Bob saw Jesus as that friend who was there to lie under a starry sky with him on a warm summer's evening.

I have heard non-Christians, like Brandon—a beautiful young gay man I had the privilege of meeting—talk about Jesus showing up in his prayer life and how that personal and embodied connection to God was both a surprise and a gift to him. Brandon didn't have any particular notion of what Jesus would or should look like, but somehow he recognized him.

Indigenous leaders in our Church have been coura-geously calling for the decolonization of the Church—for a true, self-determining Indigenous expression of our Anglican Church. They recognize that so much of their relationship with the Church has been forced on them, particularly at the expense of their own language and traditional teachings. Part of the rav-ages of the genocide they have endured has been the dislocation of their people from the belief systems that have always informed and guided their people. And yet, these leaders want to recon-nect with Indigenous teachings within the Christian faith, and therefore within the Church. They could simply leave, but instead they are staying and claiming their own God-given place in the Church and in the Church's leadership. That's not because of how good the Church has been to them. It's because they experience how Jesus is embodied in them too. They see how the face of God is also Indigenous.

When the disciples began to encounter the risen Jesus in those first days of Easter, they had an enormous amount of trouble recognizing him. Mary thought he was the gardener. Cleopas and his companion on the road to Emmaus thought that Jesus was a fellow traveler hightailing it out of Jerusalem. Whether their own vision was cloudy, or whether Jesus just looked different, their lack of recognition offered a foretaste of how the resurrected Jesus is no longer just for them, how his appearance can no longer be contained.

Martha, Do You Love Me?

Joan was my spiritual director for the five years that I lived in Orillia. I have had several different spiritual directors because of the number of times we have moved. Audrey and Kevin and Louise have offered me spiritual direction that Anne of Green Gables would describe as that of kindred spirits. They have ministered to me as people who understand and relate to the things that are most central to who I am spiritually. Joan wasn't like that. She had a very different way of relating to God than I do, and she would demand to know things about me in ways that could only be described as intrusive. She was unafraid to call into question the way I prayed, ministered, and practiced self-care. It ended up being extremely important and helpful direction at that time in my life, even if I had to learn when to be humbled enough to do some legitimate soul-searching and when to push back and stand up for myself.

Joan once asked me if I ever told Jesus that I loved him. I was unnerved by the question and said so. It seemed cringy to imagine my prayer to Jesus containing the words "I love you"—like next I'm going to be singing some awful country song about my Savior boyfriend. But it was a question that stayed with me long after that time together and long after I moved away and no longer saw Joan for spiritual direction. Of course I love Jesus. When I describe the spiritual awakening of my mid-teens, when I discerned my calling to be a priest, I can only say that I fell in love with Jesus. But saying that to Jesus had never occurred to me.

Pádraig Ó Tuama is an Irish Christian writer. He describes in his book *In the Shelter* working as a chaplain for a year at a retreat center that saw young people, mostly tweens and early teens, coming through for day retreats on a regular basis. He would invite these young people to imagine walking with Jesus, and then they would discuss what they saw and talked about in this imaginative prayer. The students reported a whole variety of ways of seeing and hearing Jesus. What is striking about Pádraig's reporting of these students' conversations with Jesus is how real and unaffected they sound. He writes:

> Another student said, "When Jesus knew my name, it felt normal. When I could say anything to him, I asked him how he was." The reciprocality of this encounter, so easily accepted, and so easily offered, was surprising because it is so often absent from much religious rhetoric, the aim for which is often to prove an ideological point about Jesus of Nazareth, rather than engage with him.[1]

A common reason for not believing in Jesus is it is too complicated. This is part of what I think people are getting at when they say that they are "spiritual, not religious." They believe in God, a higher power, perhaps a vague Creator. The specificity of Jesus, however, is a step too far. Likewise, my fellow parishioners can all mostly get on board with the Jesus who is a great guy, inspiring teacher, even a healer and miracle-worker. But in every study that I have ever led at any church, there is always a handful of people who want to leave it at that. They argue that in naming Jesus as God, we lose sight of the human being to whom we can actually relate, who invites us to follow in his footsteps, and who makes that invitation seem possible because Jesus is like us.

But the reciprocity that Ó Tuama names is where belief in Jesus ultimately gets its legs. Jesus rarely shows up looking like a first-century Galilean but most definitely shows up in the people who cross our paths each and every day. The invitation in all of this showing up is to know how God loves us, loves us personally,

---

1 Pádraig Ó Tuama, *In the Shelter* (London: Hodder & Stoughton, 2015), 69.

loves us at the core of the unique people that we actually are. That's the important point: engaging with this one who comes to us as a face that we both do and don't recognize and who companions and heals and challenges and loves us.

And who we also learn to love in return.

DISCUSSION QUESTIONS

1. This chapter begins with the image of Jesus as dirty feet. Do you have an image of Jesus with which you particularly connect? Is there a story of Jesus, or a spiritual encounter with Jesus, that is particularly powerful for you?

2. Why might it be important that Jesus shows up as "a face that we do and don't recognize"?

3. Do you tell Jesus you love him? Do you express your love for God? We talk a lot about God's love for us. Why might it be important for us to express our love in return?

CHAPTER 11

God Will Cut You Down (and That's a Good Thing)

You Can Run on for a Long Time

I am a part of a small group with a circle of wise, prayerful, honest women. Krista was leading the group one morning and asked us to consider the gospel call at the center of our lives—to continually and intentionally orient ourselves toward Jesus.

"Do you have red flags?" she asked. "Are there things that you have to watch out for that tell you that you've gotten off track? What tells you that you've gotten far away from Jesus?"

A few of the women talked about busyness and how the demands of life left them spiritually bankrupt. Others talked about worry and anxiety and how soul destroying it was when they were trapped into feeling like the weight of the world rested on their shoulders.

I have gotten far away from Jesus in my busyness and worry, but that's not my typical spiritual pitfall. In general, I feel more connected when my plate is full to overflowing and when I'm dealing with challenges that I don't feel equipped to manage. Those are the times in my life that tend to offer spiritual clarity for me. Any illusion that I might have that I can navigate life on my own falls away. I have no other option than to lean on God, to draw on wisdom and strength that comes from outside of myself.

My red flag is arrogance. As a chronic overachiever, it is all too easy for me to get caught up in my own press, to feel like my achievements and successes define and protect me. I can get myself perched on top of some pretty high horses of thinking I have the mysteries of life all figured out—and I've got the accolades and affirmations to prove it.

This particular red flag is not always successful at drawing me back to Jesus. But it is often a signal that my position on that high horse is precarious and that I'm going to topple off of it in due course. The great thing about that inevitable toppling is that God is patient, loving, and faithful—not just when I'm living my best spiritual life, but also when I'm sprawled in the dust.

There is a song that I find helpful in these moments. It's a traditional, but I know it as a Johnny Cash song. Dan and I purchased Cash's late-life, stripped-down masterpiece, *American V: A Hundred Highways*, in 2006 at a stop on our first cross-Canada road trip. We were driving out of the flat Calgary terrain, with the prairie provinces stretching out in front of us on a road that felt like it was never-ending, when Cash's voice growled through our car speakers:

> You can run on for a long time
> Sooner or later, God'll cut you down.

I was immediately drawn in by Cash's dark and threatening tone. When I hear the song still, I feel like that same very small person with the skies opening up all around me and the road going on forever.

Something else opens in me too. For any of us who have known what it is to be backed into a corner of our own making, we can't help, deep down, to long for the possibility that God's terrifying redemption could actually set us free. That freedom must be connected to the song's inherent promise: we're not in this alone. We can get pretty far along the road of self-reliance, but we can't outrun the relationships on which our lives are grounded.

Not that we aren't given every opportunity to try.

Our level of material wealth and the fast-paced nature of technology make religion and community seem quaint and unnecessary in today's world. More importantly, I am relentlessly shoehorned into believing that a reasonable goal in life is to keep for myself what I, myself, have. I am sold skin creams to keep my face from getting wrinkles. I am sold insurance policies so that all that I currently have will be protected in the case of disaster striking. I am sold diets and health fads so that I can "maintain" or "get back" my figure. I am sold ever-shifting advice on how to stay healthy, this holy grail held out to me, promising that death and decline can be held at bay . . . if I just eat the right number of vegetable servings and get on the most recent bandwagon of the right cooking oil.

I'm not condemning insurance or skin cream or healthy lifestyles. But when I am primed to think that this life is about guarding myself, it becomes difficult to imagine that there might be anything outside this religious pursuit of my own maintenance. Sometimes, though, the lie of it all catches up. Sometimes I can't run any further. Sometimes it all comes crashing down.

Out of the Heat

In the hot and sweaty summer of 2019, our church community got stuck on one topic of conversation, and it was a thorny one. Our parish council had agreed to offer space to a temporary shelter seven nights a week through July and August called Out of the Heat. The program was eye-opening, though at the time I would have said that we at St. George's didn't especially need to have our eyes opened. We have offered a daily free neighborhood breakfast for decades. We are familiar with those living on poverty's edge in our downtown. Yet none of us really had any idea that a mat in our gymnasium would be the only option for so many people to find a safe place to sleep at night. None of us realized just how great the need was in the core of our small city.

Our staff spent that summer picking up more opioid needles from our property and calling more ambulances for suspected overdoses than can be imagined. Our caretaker, Johan, had to cut back the shrubbery all around the church building in order to discourage people from pooing in the bushes. The number of guests at our daily breakfast program more than doubled, straining those resources—the volunteers' time and commitment, not to mention the money required to run the program—to the breaking point. Out of the Heat ended in the morning and spilled out into our parking lot, where we rented parking spaces to help support our programs. Our staff began doing double duty as makeshift security, taking on the unforgiving and unending task of trying to get people to move out of the parking lot so the cars paying for the spaces could park. Not only were these requests sometimes met with outbursts that left our staff concerned for their personal safety, we also felt a heavy burden of guilt in having to do so. People had nowhere else to go once breakfast wrapped up. We could clearly see the variety of illnesses—mental and physical—that were plaguing our overnight guests, and yet we had only the faintest idea of how we might be able to help.

Our church is one of the most beautiful and historic buildings in all of St. Catharines. The conversation that Out of the Heat sparked was one of great hand-wringing because the program was creating both a blight on that beauty and a serious threat to the safety of our staff and parishioners. Out of the Heat became the target of outrage as calls came from across the community to disband it. At the heart of the outrage was an appealing idea: once Out of the Heat was gone, everything would return to normal. And yet, short of moving our church into a gated community, these problems weren't going to magically disappear. Since we couldn't build gates and fences or move out of downtown, that outrage forced us to see some things with a new clarity.

The level of need in our downtown screamed to us that the system was failing far too many people. Putting our heads into the sand of our individual spheres of self-concern was not an option. Even from our calmer neighborhoods and our middle-class homes, it became impossible to make believe that we didn't have a share in these problems.

More Than Space

The Anglican Church of Canada has been profoundly blessed now for many years by the faithful leadership of Indigenous people who have tenaciously continued to walk with us, despite our historically and continuously causing them so much harm. They have been willing to pursue reconciliation with the colonial church, even though we really have no right to ask them to. Similar stories of reconciliation and blessing are being negotiated all across the world with determined and generous leaders from historically marginalized communities refusing to give up on the truth of who the church really is. In their faithfulness and their leadership, they help the whole church to better see and be who we really are.

From the Indigenous Canadian Church has come hard-earned wisdom. Several of our Canadian Indigenous communities have made global news headlines when waves of youth suicides have marked them as the highest suicide rates per capita anywhere on the planet. Every one of our Church's Indigenous leaders has not just had to be versed in scripture and theology, but also in suicide prevention and addiction, grief, and trauma counseling.

There has been a tendency in the colonial church to imagine that what we really need on the road to reconciliation is to give Indigenous people the space to "be themselves." We've been working for a long time toward self-determination in our Church, building in the structures that allow Indigenous people to make decisions in ways that are consistent with their own traditions and cultural norms.

A grave delusion is baked into this approach. First of all, we can't simply quarter off part of our Church, and part of our country, and imagine that if we give them space, the rest of us can just continue going about our regular business. Second of all, to attempt to do so is to miss out.

Indigenous leaders of our Church have fiercely named the suicide and addiction crises in their communities as spiritual crises. And what they have learned is that the commonly accepted methodology of connecting individual people with the available supports and resources doesn't work. These spiritual traumas require communal interventions. What needs to be strengthened and attended to most are relationships. People need to reconnect to one another in healthy ways, and they need to feel rooted to the earth and to the one who created that earth. One of the most successful suicide prevention programs currently offered is a youth music program, first piloted at Six Nations near Brantford, Ontario.

It isn't enough to just give Indigenous people the space to tend to themselves and learn their own lessons. I am troubled by any language that suggests that it's time to affirm Indigenous leadership in order to right past wrongs. Of course, we do need to right past wrongs and create space. But also, we need to pay attention. We need to see Indigenous leaders as leaders. Period. We need to hear their story as one that affects all of us, that has hard-earned knowledge and wisdom we all need to hear. The crises we continue to witness in downtown St. Catharines are not disconnected from those of the First Peoples. We are also in spiritual crisis. And we also need communal solutions.

My Heart Is a Gated Community Too

These communal solutions need to start at the level of changing our hearts. This is the ultimate spiritual trick: pride. It is said to be the greatest sin, the biggest barrier to relationship with God. It is certainly the biggest barrier to relationship with one another. In a million different ways, we trick ourselves into thinking that we stand alone, that we go it alone, that we are self-sufficient, that we don't need. We get so fooled into thinking this that sometimes when our self-sufficiency comes crashing down—and it always will, because we can't and don't stand alone, we do make mistakes, we get sick, and we will each die—we think that all is lost and that we have nowhere to turn.

The status quo sets up shop in the gated community of my heart as well. I make believe that this life is about doing what I want; I just need to follow my desires; I am in charge of my own destiny; my worldview is the one that represents the truth. I get up on my high horse, and no matter how bright the red flag that is waving at me while I'm up there, I forget that the fall from that precarious perch is inevitable.

It's the urgency of Johnny Cash's song that sounds most hopeful to me. Our false idols will crumble one way or the other. Mistakes, heartbreaks, illness, mortality—it will all catch up with us. The dire need of our world will crash through those gates. Our beautiful edifices will be confronted by the ugliness we so want to ignore.

A Step

Out of the Heat ended on the last night of August 2019. On the first day of September, a Sunday, our parking lot was strewn with debris, makeshift tents, shopping carts full of each individual's worldly goods. Some of the unhoused population had already started to migrate toward the park to claim a place to sleep under the trees until November, hoping for a mild autumn as they waited for the next temporary shelter to open. Even if we had wanted to extend the program at our church, a number of threatening letters from the city, which was suddenly concerned with a set of dusty bylaws that this shelter had been breaking, prohibited us from doing so. We had to ask those still lingering on our property to clean up and leave.

That fall we opened the doors of a newly renovated part of our church to offer counseling and mentorship to the struggling youth in our city in a center we call Step. I had the great fortune of working with a gifted leader, Suzanne, to take on our little germ of an idea of how we might respond to the dire needs we were seeing and make it into a living, breathing offering to our community. It has been amazing to watch others across our church and city come on board to help shape the vision and reality of what Step is and can be. At the core of Step is the hunch that the most important thing we could offer to the need around us was ourselves. We seek to respond to the struggles of our city's young people with a circle of care, with the offering of community and relationship.

The spiritual crisis in us, and in the world—it's real. The church that, like it or not, is the polar opposite of being a gated community, is itself a response to that spiritual crisis. Its identity is based in reconnecting what has become disconnected: us to one another, our human family to God. You can run on for a long time, but sooner or later God will cut you down. The reason why this is such good news is because when it has all been pulled apart, what's left is at least real.

DISCUSSION QUESTIONS

1. Do you have a spiritual red flag? Are there patterns or behaviors that consistently draw you away from God?

2. We are taught that this life is about holding on to what we already have. How do you experience this to be true? Why is this a problem?

3. We can't outrun our relational truth, nor can we outrun God. Martha notes that this is freeing. What is good about being confronted again with the truth of how connected our lives really are?

4. The church is an answer to our spiritual disconnection, a witness to how our lives are actually bound to one another and to God. How does the church serve the world out of this truth?

CHAPTER 12

Truth Will Not Remain Unseen

Mary and Martha

My mom had a Bible verse laminated for me when I started out in ministry, and it hangs as a reminder above my desk: "Martha, Martha, you are worried and distracted by many things. There is need of only one thing." It comes from that often-repeated story of Jesus eating in the home of Mary and Martha. Martha was busy preparing the supper and got annoyed with her sister, Mary, for not helping out, for acting like one of Jesus's male disciples, sitting in on her teacher's lesson rather than taking her place in the kitchen as she was expected to do.

I can relate to different parts of this story, depending on my mood and where God most needs to speak into my life in any given moment. I love this story as a feminist and as a person who isn't keen on housework. I would always rather learn, read, listen, debate, and engage in conversation than attend to the dusting. I hear Jesus affirming a surprising place for women in his ministry, honoring the inquiring and discerning heart of his dear disciple Mary. I hear a lot of love for Martha too, for her task-oriented ways and for the value that "doing" can play in the kingdom of God. Martha, we know from John's Gospel, was also keenly insightful about who Jesus was, and she articulated her faith in him in a concise and piercing way. I hear in Mary and Martha's story the good news that women contain multitudes.

Sometimes I hear a corrective, which is why I keep that scripture passage above my desk. Sometimes what I most need is to be called away from the worry and the tasks to the relationship with Jesus.

Mostly what I experience in this story, though, is that I am seen. I am seen in *my* multitudes and complexities, in the variety of ways that I love and serve God, in the many and particular ways I am called back into God's loving service.

I also experience in this story how we are seen, how there is room made for all of us. There isn't just one right way of knowing and serving God. There isn't just a male way, or a white way, or a heterosexual way. We don't serve just by learning and praying at our Lord's feet, and the body of Christ isn't just made up of those who get the job done. There is difference and diversity in this thing we call church.

Of course, we can also reciprocate. We can also get better at allowing God to be seen. We can make and hold space for the God who makes and holds space for us.

Instagram Face

I have a guilty love for The Bachelor reality television show franchise. I wouldn't be quite as addicted to it if it weren't for the Bachelor podcast that I get to listen to after each show, where feminists Emma Gray and Claire Fallon "lovingly snark" on every maddening moment between the lead and the various love interests of each season. The show's premise is ridiculous: select one man or woman, cast thirty potential suitors for them to weed through, and, at the end, the lead picks one of the contestants to marry. Baked into that premise are certain assumptions, particularly around gender roles, heteronormative relationships, and the buffed, tanned, toned, wrinkle- and wobble-free bodies that represent one very lucrative template for beauty.

Emma and Claire love to rail against the fact that each season the contestants skew younger and younger. The younger they are, the more uniform and Instagram-worthy their beauty becomes. It is increasingly clear that the most likely outcome from being cast on any of the Bachelor franchise shows is not love, but rather to become a social media influencer. To be cast on the show is to be granted access to a direct pipeline of profitable numbers of online followers.

Jia Tolentino writes in a *New Yorker* article "The Age of Instagram Face" about this increasingly homogenized beauty aes-
thetic, its connection to social media, and the ravenous beauty
industry (particularly the plastic surgery industry) that has grown
in response to people's desire to look a certain way: "[There has
arisen] the gradual emergence, among professionally beautiful
women, of a single, cyborgian face. It's a young face, of course,
with poreless skin and plump, high cheekbones. It has catlike eyes
and long, cartoonish lashes; it has a small, neat nose and full, lush
lips. . . . A face that looks like it's made out of clay."[1]

The Bachelor represents the impulse toward what I like to
call the Designer Community. It is hardly a new phenomenon, or
one that is merely seen on reality television. It is well documented
on the pages of scripture, down through the ages, and all across
our society today, that human societies love boundaries and defi-
nitions around our human groupings so that we know who is in
and who is out. Within the groupings of who is in, we strive for a
sameness, for an ironing out of the wrinkles of difference—much
as "Instagram Face" erases the wrinkles, blemishes, and any other
unique particularities from our faces. We all then participate in
both the power of naming and maintaining those boundaries that
keep like with like, as well as succumbing to the ruling of those
boundaries, even at the expense of hiding or suppressing our own
differences in order to be able to belong.

We do this because there are a lot of comforting things about
the Designer Community. Namely, if we can negotiate the boundaries and if we can fit in well enough, if we can eliminate enough
of the appearance of difference, then the reward for individuals
who make it to the inside is belonging and identity. To know who
we are, to know that we are part of something, these address powerful human desires.

But there have also always been great financial incentives
that drive the creation of the Designer Community. *The Bachelor*

1 Jia Tolentino, "The Age of Instagram Face," The New Yorker, December 12, 2019, https://www.newyorker.com/culture/decade-in-review/
the-age-of-instagram-face.

reality television show is emblematic of a dynamic that is age-old. When we are relentlessly marketed one standardized image of beauty and worthiness, when that one image is idealized and fetishized to the point that we can't help but want it for ourselves too, then we are primed to be excellent consumers. We can be sold a whole variety of products that promise to nudge us closer to that ideal. Inherent in the promise of reaching that ideal are those same age-old, perpetually desirable promises of identity and belonging.

Jesus Formed the Church to be the Anti-Designer Community

We pour energy into the power structures and institutional realities of the church, but Jesus never promised to save the institution. He promised to dismantle the things that have become barriers, rather than servants, in real flesh-and-blood people coming to know God.

As these real flesh-and-blood people, we can mess up our witness to the world. We can make it harder for others to see and know the love of God. And God can show up in the cracks of our lives and our failed witness too.

We break off from one another, we fracture, and we schism as we try to secure the right version of what this is all about. And in that fracture and schism, something of the untamable, unpossessable power of God is revealed. We make God in our own image, yet God's image can only be revealed in the multicolored company of the people in whom God is at work.

We set up our gated communities in our hearts, around our churches, but God won't be held in, or out, by any gates.

We try to make the church into a Designer Community. We even create structures and rules around the church to edit out and manage difference. Yet the Lord in whom we live revealed the nearness of the kingdom of God by eating with the rejects of society. Jesus saved his most terrifying parables and most judgmental teachings for those like the rich man in the parable with Lazarus, who walk by and refuse to see themselves as related to the suffering of others. He enacted a ministry, not by himself, but with a cobbled-together assortment of desperate people—fishermen, demoniacs, widows, tax collectors, and Samaritans—out of whom he saw, named, and called forth gifts for proclaiming the kingdom of God.

The ultrareal church can't be anything other than an anti–Designer Community.

The Designer Community and the Church's Whiteness

In the summer of 2020, three female Episcopal priests of color, Kelly Brown Douglas, Stephanie Spellers, and Winnie Varghese, penned an open letter to their Church on the celebration of Independence Day. They named that impulse for sameness, and they named its sinister consequences baked into the founding of America. That Designer Community—rigidly defining who will belong and who will be privileged—has been intentionally constructed in America around the centering of whiteness. They write, "It is a culture and way of being that claims superiority and universality, even as it subjugates, appropriates, silences, deports, dehumanizes, and eliminates that which is not White."[2]

They note that there is great privilege in securing whiteness for ourselves, in being able to find ourselves defined within its constructs. White supremacy, systemic racism—these represent the Designer Community writ large. It is using the difference of skin color to decide who matters, who rules, who flourishes, whose stories get seen and shown. The problem is that this privilege is secured on the basis of excluding others from participating. The problem is that the humanity of all of us is diminished when any of us secure privilege based on keeping others out. The problem is that this systematic and privileged whiteness is not who we really are. It is a denial of truth.

The problem is that this privileging of whiteness is not just baked into the founding of America, it is also baked into the

---

2 Stephanie Spellers, "Speaking of Freedom," Medium, July 8, 2020, https://medium.com/@revsteph/speaking-of-freedom-54ad2a49eb05.

structuring of our churches. This must be called out; the church must see that this is not who we really are; the church must be called back to truth. In that same open letter to the church, Spellers, Douglas, and Varghese write: "[We] must decide whether [we are] going to be White (that is, allied with oppression) or be church. Jesus made his choice. In his crucifixion, he let-go of anything that set him apart from the crucified classes of people of his day. He understood that it is only when the least of these are able to breathe freely, that the sacred humanity of all is restored."[3]

As they so eloquently note, the church has tried, again and again, in Jesus's name to be a Designer Community, to be white instead of faithful to Jesus's path. The history of the church is littered with instances when communities of people chose the comfort of a social club or of tightly monitored gates keeping the riffraff out and a reassuring sameness within. The history of the church is tainted with the violence of its leaders willingly choosing to edit out those who were thought to threaten the institution with their differences. These are tragic manifestations of an impulse that is all too ordinary, an impulse that I see in my own faith community. And in myself too.

In our daily breakfast program, our Step youth resource center offering counseling to youth living on the margins, and in the temporary overnight shelter we have hosted, it can often all feel like too much. Sometimes the mental illness, the shouting and hallucinating that happens in our parking lot in the middle of the night that disrupts the neighbors, the vandalism to our property and to our vehicles parked in the church's lot, the drug paraphernalia littered across our property, the people passed out in our bushes or camping out in our memorial garden—sometimes it all feels like too much. There are, of course, times when we would rather retreat into the safety of a gated community, either figuratively or literally, and shut our doors on the problems that, let's be honest, we don't have a hope in hell of ultimately solving. Sometimes, we wish we could just worship our God in peace.

---

3 Ibid.

Thankfully, the blessing of the poor, the meek, the down-trodden, the grieving, the brokenhearted, the addicted, and the hallucinating keep breaking into that Designer Community inclination, just as Jesus promised.

Thankfully, the history of the church isn't just littered with instances of our getting it wrong. It is also showered with the inconvenient blessing of God—God the whirlwind, God the lightning and thunder, God the stranger, God the hungry and imprisoned and sick and naked, God the crucified.

Truth Will Not Remain Unseen

This is a story of God the Creator breaking into our Designer Community impulse and calling us back to our true identity as the church. This is a story that brings this second part of the book full circle. It's a story of brokenness. It's a story of God's breaking into the cracks of our lives, no matter how we might try to put the safety brake on our experience of the holy. It's a story about the prayer and praise of the church—not as it might be, but as it actually is. It's a mess. It's not just for us. And it matters. It matters that we see our worship and our community of worship for what it really is and who it is really for. It's a story that can't be anything other than living and life-giving. It's a story of the ultrareal church.

Advent Café is the name for our evening midweek service. We call it Advent Café because we understand that the Advent call to wake up and to watch expectantly for the coming of our Lord carries through the whole year and into every part of our lives.

Before the pandemic, Advent Café was held in the same room we use for our Sunday coffee hour, and it operated the same night as Out of the Cold, which was hosted in the gymnasium just below, offering a meal—and at times an overnight shelter—for whoever showed up to be fed. Although some of our regular Sunday attendees came out for Advent Café too, there were also, as we had hoped, people who found that the timing, the location, and the format of this service allowed them a way into church that Sunday morning hadn't afforded. Numerous Out of the Cold guests have become a regular part of Advent Café. They arrived for the hot meal downstairs and then made their way through the Memorial Garden to join us for worship. They are valued people in our community.

One Wednesday, we were two songs into worship when one of our Advent Café attendees, I'll call her Jane, became distressed. At first, she was having a coughing fit. Our greeter for the evening quietly fetched a bottle of water from the fridge as we continued on with the service. Business as usual, however, quickly became impossible. When it appeared that she was having difficulty breathing and her coughing turned into great heaving, panicked gasps for air, we stopped the music and called 911.

It turns out that someone had lit a cigarette in the hallway right outside the door and Jane was having a bad reaction to the tobacco smoke. I got one of our parishioners, Tom, to come with me, and we went out to ask the smoker to stop. The man we found outside was not only smoking but had also created for himself a little drug den. He was sprawled on the floor with the offending cigarette in his mouth, and scattered all around him were baggies and needles. I asked him to put out his cigarette, and he ignored me, unable or unwilling to hear. I explained the situation and reached over to take the cigarette out of his fingers, assuming that he was too inebriated to be able to respond. He became angry and tried to slap me away, but his reflexes were heavy and uncoordinated.

I was at a loss. Jane was still gasping for air inside. The cigarette was still burning. The paramedics were on their way, and this man had the hallway entirely blocked and showed at least the potential of being dangerous.

Ryan came out into the hallway from the service just then. He is part of our Advent Café congregation. He also regularly attends Out of the Cold and St. George's breakfast program. I watched with awe as Ryan, with calm expertise, reached through the haze of this man's drug-induced stupor, helped him extinguish his cigarette, and gather up his things. Then he gently walked him down the stairs. Shortly afterward, six paramedics arrived and began the rather lengthy process of calming down Jane's breathing. We eventually resumed worship. Our prayers were informed by the needs we had witnessed that night and with gratitude for the skill and compassion of the paramedics who responded to our call for help.

The next morning, I arrived at the church just as Ryan was coming out from breakfast. "Thank you," I enthused. "You were amazing. You were able to talk to that man when nobody else could. You were so calm and kind and understanding. You really defused a difficult situation."

"Yeah," he sighed in response. "I just felt so bad after. I should have invited that guy in to our service. I was so concerned about getting him out of the way, and I didn't even think that maybe what he really needed was to join us."

"Oh," I said with surprise. "I didn't think of that."

"I know, right?" he said sadly. "I mean, that's what the church is here for."

I left Ryan and went into my office, shut the door, and cried. They could have been tears of regret and guilt for having missed the opportunity to see a fellow brother and to invite him in to our community rather than merely packing him up and getting him out of the way. But instead, my tears were shed with gladness. That's what the church is here for.

I am glad to be part of an identity like that. I am glad for Ryan to understand something more fully than I do and to share that knowledge with me. I am glad that this Advent promise of God's ongoing presence and activity in our lives is true. I am glad to be startled into a new wakefulness by the voice of my Lord.

DISCUSSION QUESTIONS

1. The Designer Community constructs our relationships with one another around editing out difference. Where do you see the reality of Designer Communities at work? How does that impulse for sameness manifest itself in your life?

② The ultrareal church is not a Designer Community. It is the "multicolored company of heaven." God sees and loves and welcomes us in our diversity and difference. Where have you been challenged or blessed by the diversity and difference of God's community?

③ In the story that closes this chapter, Ryan understands in a profound way who the church really is and what the church is for. What is compelling to you about Ryan's story?

III

Acceptance— How the Community of Faith Reveals the Power of God

CHAPTER 13

Maybe Time Running Out Is a Gift

No Pause Button

Cecilia decided that they wanted to get their septum pierced for their fourteenth birthday.

"No way," both Dan and I said. This was not one we had to think about. Cecilia had talked about a nose piercing, which both of us had reluctantly agreed could happen before they began high school. I had pictured a tasteful, barely-there sparkle on the side of a nostril. I hadn't thought of a great big colorful ring hanging through the middle of the nose that seemed not so far removed from being pressed up against my body as they were nursing.

Fierce is a word we have always used to describe Cecilia. Determined would be another. Although their first reaction to our no was to accuse us of being bad parents and then storm up to their room, they eventually came up with careful, calm, and well-thought-out arguments to each of our oppositions. I did what I normally do: I talked it out. I was going into the church the next day, so I shared the conundrum with Scott, Brad, and Matt—our livestream worship crew at St. George's—and asked that they weigh in.

"You were right to say no," Matt said.

"Has she thought about the cultural implications of what she's doing?" Scott asked. "Does she know what it means?"

"You might encourage secrecy if you don't let her," Brad said. "There isn't any lasting harm, is there?"

"Maybe Brad is right," Matt waffled.

Around this time a certain reality set in: there is no pause button. That's an obvious statement. It applies to life, not just parenting. When the kids were young, people constantly told me,

"Treasure every moment; it all goes by so quickly." When we were in the midst of diapers and temper tantrums and trying to navigate sleep schedules and pureed food and spit-up, it didn't feel like life was moving too fast. And yet, I don't remember the last time that I was able to sweep either of my children up into my arms, feeling their precious weight nuzzle into me. I would have liked to have treasured that moment with each of them, and it slipped past without my noticing.

We have lost loved ones, and we thought that our lives would not go on without their being with us. We have moved more than once, and each time it has felt as if we would never get over having to leave the places and people behind that had come to define home and friendship for us in such important ways. We said goodbye to our difficult and beloved dog Cliff Barnes, swearing that we would never subject our hearts to this kind of loss again, only to then find ourselves ready to welcome not one but two new puppies into our family just a few years later.

Suddenly, here we were, debating with our soon-to-be-four-teen-year-old on whether they could get a ring put through the center of their nose. Around the same time, Gordon, just twelve, grew about two feet and was suddenly looking me in the eye when we talked. His voice changed to a hearty baritone.

Brad's advice and Cecilia's determination won out. Dan and I said yes to the septum piercing.

If We Had All the Time in the World

"Maybe time running out is a gift," Jason Isbell sings in his achingly beautiful song "If We Were Vampires." He begins the song naming specific details he treasures about his wife, the talented singer-songwriter Amanda Shires, and then he notes that what makes these small things about her all the more meaningful is the knowledge that it is so fleeting. "If we were vampires"—if we were immortal, if we had all of the time in the world—we might be careless with our lives and loves. I hear in these lyrics the insight that there is an important blessing in the fact that our lives don't come with a pause button.

I read an essay long ago, written by Laurie Lee and shared by Bruce Iserman, my high school English teacher, that provided a vision of heaven. He described many of the gentle, warm, and lovely images we would associate with paradise. But he included in his description a hint of sadness, a shadow of regret, that small ache in the chest or catch in the throat, that speak to what it all costs, how precious and fleeting it is, and how we have been created with the ability of naming both love and loss. It is in that tension where ecstasy is found. Heaven has to include that ache.

Jason Isbell and Laurie Lee provide a different perspective on death than the message we normally receive. With disappointing consistency, I hear death talked about almost as an embarrassment, as if a person's body and mind falling apart is not just a physical failing, but perhaps a sort of moral failing too. We worry about dignity in dying, and in Canada we are now legally able to engineer the time and place of a quick, easy, sanitized death, which we are made to believe affords us that desperately desired dignity. Dignity, we understand, comes from maintaining our lives on our own terms, not becoming overly pathetic or needy, not burdening the people around us unduly.

"God works because of who we are, not in spite of who we are" was the hashtag-worthy refrain of Brian Ruttan, one of my seminary professors. Despite the fact that he said it in almost every one of our lessons, when it came up at exam time, a handful of people still got marks taken off for not getting it. Although we speak often as Christians of God's grace, it remains hard to believe that even the most pathetic and fragile things about our human lives could actually be part and parcel of how God is at work in the world.

And yet, if God doesn't meet us in death, God has nothing to offer us.

Death Isn't Pretty

Death isn't pretty. It isn't romantic. It robs us of the people and things we love the most. It strips us of our faculties, our function, our purpose, our minds. Death can break us in ways that leave us bitter and brittle. Death is also the starting place for our Christian life. Far from shying away from the ugliness of how this all ends, Christians lean into it.

I said that Jesus was acutely aware that the community he called into existence was going to be full of people. I have noted that Jesus was under no illusions about this mess that he chose to be the vehicle of how his life will continue into the world. As we saw in the last section of this book, the mess is kind of the point. This is the acceptance to which I invite the church: we are a collection of fractures across our human relationships; we are the invitation to keep figuring out how to love and serve one another. We are also people in whom the power of God will be revealed— not in spite of who we are, but because of it.

When asked how many times we are to forgive one another, Jesus tells his followers, "not seven times, but seventy times seven times." Seventy times seven is a number that speaks to God's activity. Seven is the number of fulfillment and wholeness. It's God's number. And it is also our number. It's the bringing together of heaven and earth, the overcoming of each and every divide. It's the number of our redemption, and it's only possible through God. That's why we don't have to be embarrassed about death, we don't have to just get over our grief, we don't have to minimize our losses, we don't have to pretend away the glaring gaps of who and what is no longer with us. We can both lament and celebrate the fact that life doesn't come with a pause button. Our lament speaks of our gratitude. And our celebration looks expectantly for God's promises to meet us right here, where it all falls apart.

Jesus is the in-the-flesh revelation of the God who doesn't shy away from the heartbroken mess that is our lives and, in fact, is committed to working in and through that mess as God's chosen vehicle for how love will be made known. It's in God's commitment to being at work through the mess that is also how our mess gets redeemed, how beauty and goodness and forgiveness and healing do get revealed in and through us, how a communion does get established between us that even death can't break.

The stories in part III take place exactly here—in the disappointments, the suffering and illness, the face-to-face encounters with evil, in the dead and dying places of our lives. In ultrarealism, we are asked to come to grips with exactly the circumstances of the right now, the ultrareal of who and what we are.

From that place of understanding, our next step is acceptance. If part II helped us to see who we are, then what we need in that move to acceptance is the grace of God. We can accept who we are when we learn to see the God who could be revealed to us because of the mess and fragility and heartbreak, not in spite of it.

Nothing Can Make Up for the Loss

When we went into lockdown in mid-March 2020, I had a naive idea of what was before us. Even a few weeks seemed like a long time to be away from the worship, celebration, prayer, lament, song, and fellowship that is the life of the church. As each date we planned as a community came and went and had to be postponed, we started saying to one another, "It will be so good when we can be back together again!" I imagined the church filled, our favorite hymns being sung; I pictured the gladness with which we would greet one another, the stories and hugs that would be shared. I was sure we would dig in to a classic Soup Sunday—St. George's favorite soup and homemade bread reception—after the service. We would definitely eat cake.

When we did briefly reopen for in-person worship in the fall of 2020, it was nothing like I had imagined. We had online registrations, carefully controlled seating arrangements, radically diminished and scattered numbers, not to mention such rigidly choreographed patterns of movement that a measuring tape became our best friend for figuring out how to invite people to come up for communion. The pandemic was still raging, which meant that many of our people—for so many good reasons— chose to remain at home. Barriers were everywhere: masks, physical distance, traffic flow, clean-up crews. This meant that being able to even smile at my parishioners, let alone reach out and embrace them or talk to them, was almost impossible.

I didn't calculate the cumulative cost of death either. Two weeks before reopening, one of the saints of our church, the feisty force of nature that was Dorothy Dundas, died after a brief non-COVID illness. She was one of what became a staggering number of beloved parishioners who died before we could be back together again. Each of these deaths hit our community hard. And each one was even more difficult to process without the usual rituals upon which we depend. We couldn't visit our dear ones as they died; we couldn't hold their family in our arms. In most cases we could only gather in the smallest of numbers to honor and celebrate them, and many chose to wait on any gathering at all.

At Dorothy's funeral, just two days before reopening, I shared these words from Dietrich Bonhoeffer to name the reality of the Dorothy-shaped hole now part of our community. I shared it again at that first strange Sunday when we were back to some stilted version of in-person worship:

> Nothing can make up for the absence of someone whom we love; we must simply hold out and see it through. That sounds very hard at first, but at the same time it is a great consolation, for the gap, as long as it remains unfilled, preserves the bonds between us. It is nonsense to say that God fills the gap; God doesn't fill it, but on the contrary, keeps it empty and so helps us to keep alive our former communion with each other, even at the cost of pain.[1]

What Bonhoeffer offers in these words is hope. He is not rose-tinting anything or sweeping the reality of grief under any carpets. But he is saying that in being honest about what we have actually lost, there is grace. There is something that God makes possible in the honest-to-goodness gaps of our lives.

---

1 Dietrich Bonhoeffer, *Works*, vol. 8: *Letters and Papers from Prison* (Minneapolis: Fortress, 2009), letter no. 89, page 238.

It was difficult worshipping together in-person in the midst of COVID protocols. The glaring losses were the thing most obvious to me in our gathering. And yet, as we leaned into the weirdness with one another, as we smiled with our eyes because our masks covered our mouths, as we negotiated our movements around one another with exceptional care, as we experimented with what it felt like to hear just one person lift our songs of praise for all of us, as we sanitized and sanitized and sanitized again, as we didn't touch because that's how we had to reach out, and as we still were so very aware of how much we actually need the Holy Spirit to bring us together, exactly what Bonhoeffer named was revealed to us too. That there is a communion with one another being offered and even strengthened, particularly as we give up any pretense that any of it is easy or that any of it is possible without God.

The amazing thing about being in a church's sanctuary is that it can make alive this communion in a way that is rarely so powerfully possible anywhere else. Dorothy, and all of the others that we lost, were with us as we so awkwardly figured out how to gather again. Their faithfulness, prayer, and service left a mark on our community, and they left a mark on our space too. That spiritual energy does soak into the fabric of our bricks and mortar in a way that is easy to feel and hard to explain.

When that first favorite hymn of the morning was offered, I could just about hear those dear voices joining in the chorus of heaven. I am certain they were singing a little more loudly to make up for the fact that the rest of us couldn't sing.

DISCUSSION QUESTIONS

1. "God works because of who we are, not in spite of who we are." What does this statement mean to you?

2. "Time running out is a gift." Why might our mortality, the reality of our death and fragility, be a source of blessing?

3. Bonhoeffer says that God holds the gaps between us and our lost loved ones open in order to maintain our communion with one another, even at the cost of pain. Why is this important to know about grief? How do you experience that ongoing communion even with those who have died?

4. Why is it so important that God be able to meet us in the difficult and dying places of our lives? What resources does our Christian faith offer us in coming to terms with death?

CHAPTER 14

"We Didn't Choose This"

Always Do Your Best

On a warm summer's afternoon, I was meandering around town with newborn Gordon in his stroller, and I emerged long enough from my new mother haze to read a local church's front sign displaying a weekly slogan to tantalize passersby with a bite-sized piece of Christian gospel.

"Always Do Your Best," the sign said.

I snorted and thought to myself that the inspiration of the Holy Spirit was blowing through this congregation a little weakly if that milk-toast proclamation was all they could cobble together. As I continued home, the words began not just to amuse, but to rankle. Reducing the gospel to a slogan almost always leads to a misconstruing of the message, with potentially disastrous consequences. The Lord who comes engaging us in fiery conversation and deep self-reflection, who invites us to acts of service meant to turn the world upside down, doesn't actually boil down into neatly packaged, rhyme-off-the-top-of-your-head tidbits. The slogans that I see casually proclaimed outside of our churches mostly serve as a reminder of just how easy it is to make God into our own image.

"Always do your best" was a phrase my parents used often. They offered it as reassurance of their unconditional love, the reminder that my placing first in whatever test I was doing or music festival I was competing in was beside the point. It was their encouragement to embrace the experience, to feel good about the thing I was doing rather than focusing on the result or achievement.

I turned "Always do your best" into something different. I figured that since "my best" was almost always first place, if I fell short it was because I was in some way lacking. I became a pro at

"Always do your best." I won prizes and made my parents proud and had doors opened for me. "Always do your best" got me places.

But it was a slogan that eventually caught up with me. What happens when my best is first and I place second? What happens when I place first and it's not enough? When I'm first and I'm not enough? When "my best" reveals itself as a disappointingly empty and precarious thing after all?

Here's the thing that most offended me about that sign: I can get "Always do your best" anywhere. I can buy self-help books; I can book time with a therapist; I can work out, invest in skin creams, and buy flattering fashion choices. I can read women's magazines with all kinds of helpful articles about how to maximize my mental, physical, emotional, financial, and social health. I can get insight into thousands of possibilities for being at my best, and I can present a version of myself to the world with every sort of social media filter available in order to show up as my most polished and appealing self.

What most of us need instead, deep down inside, is somewhere to go with the stuff that isn't the best at all, that's actually the worst.

Shaped by the Worst

My dear friends, sisters Cheryl and Tanya, haven't had easy lives. To hear them describe what they went through, particularly in their early years, is to wonder what kind of justice is at work in the world. It's only marginally easier to hear of their family's suffering because I know they came through it all to become two of the warmest, most genuine and inspiring people I could possibly know.

Cheryl and Tanya were born to teen parents. They had an older sister, Missy, who had severe disabilities. She was nonverbal and nonmobile. She was fed through a tube, and she and Cheryl and Tanya were bullied in school because of her challenges. Missy died a few days before Christmas when Cheryl was entering her tween years and was buried on the morning of December 24. A few months later, Cheryl was hit by a car and was airlifted to hospital, where her frightened family was told she would be in a permanent coma if she didn't die from her injuries. Cheryl miraculously pulled through. Apart from the death and injury that marked her and Tanya's growing up so dramatically, there were also court proceedings against a close family friend who had been sexually abusive toward them and broken trust in the worst sort of way. And then there were the ongoing challenges that never seemed to let up: not enough money, addiction in some of their closest family members, divorce, and the death of a whole host of relatives.

Cheryl and Tanya are both people of faith. They both made the choice themselves later in their lives to be baptized and to become part of the church. I had the exceptional blessing of being the one to baptize Tanya.

Tanya and Cheryl are people who bring their best to the world and who have lived through the worst. They will both say that who they are was as much formed by the stuff that was the worst as by anything. What we all need is a faith that speaks not just to the truth that our lives will one day end, but also that speaks to the suffering that so profoundly shapes our lives as we go. We need an alternative to "Always do your best."

A Grain of Wheat Must Die

Just after Jesus arrived in Jerusalem for the final Passover of his earthly life, some curious bystanders came up to the disciple Philip and asked to see Jesus. When they were brought to him, Jesus offered by way of greeting a seemingly random proclamation: "Very truly, I tell you, unless a grain of wheat falls into the earth and dies, it remains just a single grain; but if it dies, it bears much fruit" (Jn 12:24). Death was on Jesus's mind. New life was going to flourish in his friends and followers in the wake of his death.

But first there would be suffering.

As a child, I was horrified and also tentatively intrigued by the stories of Jesus's crucifixion. I ran out of the room crying and couldn't sleep for several nights after watching Jesus Christ Superstar and seeing (in not very vivid detail, I realize now) the horror of Jesus's death on screen rather than just reading about it in a children's Bible. I convinced myself that God would have had the power to anesthetize Jesus from the pain of what he was going through. God would have spiritually bubble-wrapped Jesus from the first whippings to the final breath so as to spare this one that God loved so much from such pain and distress.

I didn't realize that any suggestion that Jesus was just acting his way through the most human of our experiences and not really feeling them was utterly rejected by the early church. The point is that Jesus did suffer, and Jesus did die. There was not one iota of what it means to be a human being from which Jesus was spared.

Why? Jesus responded to his friends' questions about what would be born in them because of his death. But also, his suffering came to mean something to the Christian faith too. His suffering was seen as a response in some real way to ours. New life can, in God's power, be born out of death, but it hurts like hell. How can one more suffering creature, even the Son of God, offer anything in response to that?

The image that sticks with me, that I reference regularly in sermons and in my own personal prayer life, is the image of Jesus on the cross with outstretched arms reaching across the whole aching, shattered chasm of what it is to be self-aware mortals in order to grasp me, grasp us, in the strongest of embraces and to claim us for something beautiful and true and full of life when all seems dead and destroyed. God can only be there to do that reaching, that grasping, that holding, and that claiming because God was willing to walk with us into the fullest experience of what it is to be human: to suffer, to die, to feel abandoned in our last dying breath, and to face the beyond through our limited human perspective.

My friend David reflected on an experience of our church's shared grief when the 2019 motion for Equal Marriage before our National Church's Synod was defeated by the narrowest of margins. The pain in the room that Friday night was visceral: it was a living, breathing thing. And what followed in the few days after that devastating vote was nothing short of a disaster. We were mad at each other, we were making desperate and mostly ineffective efforts to try to make amends with the LGBTQ2+ community by other sorts of legislation, we shed tears, we cursed one another, we raged. The message that was presented to the world—a world that could barely care less about what the Anglican Church is up to but will send its mainstream media to report on a vote such as this—put the Church in a decidedly terrible light.

By the end of the synod, things weren't any less messy, hearts weren't miraculously mended, but somehow we were in a different place, somehow we could see a way forward. David described the experience of grace, reconciliation, and painful new life that started to emerge in our decision-making body as God reaching "into the depths of the pain and hurt and agony and terror and death of Friday night and wresting life from the tomb. Wresting liberation from the tomb. Wresting freedom from the tomb."[1]

The companionship of God matters in a real way. People gravitate toward the poem "Footprints in the Sand" not because it is pretty or looks nice on a Hallmark card but because it describes their experience. The image it presents, of just one set of footprints during the times that are most difficult in our lives, is poignant. When we are suffering most, that is when God doesn't just walk beside us. God is carrying us.

The first time I read that poem, I cried because it rang true. That's hard to admit now, because the poem is so ridiculously commodified and overused. And yet, for so many of us who have felt cradled and carried, accompanied and befriended by the living Jesus, it resonates because we viscerally understand that Jesus's own suffering does in a very real way allow him to access, understand, and speak to my suffering as well.

And also, Jesus's redemption of our suffering matters in a real way. That doesn't mean that Jesus takes away our suffering. It also doesn't mean that somehow if we can just make it through the

---

1 David Harrison, sermon, St. Mary Magdalene, July 22nd, 2019.

difficulty then our reward is the golden prize of heaven at the end of it all.

It means that real people, through the lens and power of their Christian faith and their relationship with Jesus actually do find meaning in their suffering. If any of us had to pick whether we could be spared certain losses, of course we would pick to be spared. And also, we recognize that we could not be the people that we are today without those losses.

The Martyrs—The Witnesses

I don't understand or accept that a lot of the seemingly random horror of the world couldn't be mitigated by our loving God. I believe there is something faithful about railing against the world's gratuitous pain. I am prepared to both lament and live with that ambiguity, though, because of the martyrs. I don't mean the long-ago dead Christians who were felled in the lion's den or beheaded in the public square. I mean the people whose stories form the backbone of this book—who have shown up and shown me, shown us, what God's redemption looks and sounds like, how God really does reach across and into our pain and brokenness and "wrests life from the tomb." I mean the witnesses—which is what the word martyr literally means.

I would add James to that list of martyrs. James was a regular musical leader at our Wednesday night Advent Café service. It's a much smaller gathering, usually somewhere around thirty people, and at that time, we were holding it in the lounge of the church, so everything about the service felt more intimate. Scott—my dear friend and associate priest at the church—and his family had been going through a time of grief and upheaval. As the service that night was wrapping up, James became quite emotional. He told the group that in Christian community, there has to be honesty. In that honesty, especially when we face life's challenges and heartbreaks, we need to hold one another in prayer. This is what we're here to do. He invited us all to come forward and to lay hands on Reverend Scott and to minister to him. Together, we anointed him with the prayer James offered. And then James led us in song.

It would not be the only time that James called me back, or helped me see again, what might be a faithful response to the hurt of human life.

James died of cancer in his mid-forties. James had a strong following on social media, and he used it to share updates from diagnosis, through pain, fear, loss of mental faculties, loss of income and ability, to his final days. He shared the times of despair, as well as the times when he fiercely chose gratitude and blessing even when life was falling apart. This sharing told others that we can be honest about suffering and fear and pain, and doing so does not contradict our faith.

James didn't just post on social media, although this was a powerful offering in and of itself. He turned his story into music. Like many artistic people, James's composing had been put on the back burner because it wasn't how he was paying the bills, because he was raising a family and going to work, because when you're in that busy time of life it is normal to hardly notice the things that have been crowded out.

When James was diagnosed with incurable multiple melanoma, he started composing again. *The Lavender Fields: Living with Cancer* featured both his poetry and music, and it gave expression to the journey that starts even before you receive the news. *The Lavender Fields* debuted on April 6, 2019, in Toronto. All of us who were there in the audience that night were there with love for James and his family. We were there because we also had shared something of the shock and fear of his terrible diagnosis. We were there as another piece of the love and prayer we were seeking to offer to their family.

But we weren't just there in that audience to share in James's story. We were also there because James had dared to give voice and song to a story that wasn't just his. His music took us to those other stories of cancer, illness, and death that have touched our lives; those other thunderstruck moments when a doctor delivered the bad news to us or to a family member; those sudden recognitions of the body's capacity for betrayal, the mind's capacity for betrayal. We were there because we also knew something of what it was to have the rug of certainty and stability and predictability yanked out from underneath us, suddenly rendering the world a very different place.

Through his own story, James told us the truth of just how fragile this whole human enterprise really is. My body and the bodies of those I love are vulnerable. We get sick. We break down. We know loss. We die. We have all kinds of places in which we can be at our best, where we can learn to be, hope to be, better. But what a gift it is to be able to name the worst. What a courageous thing it is to insist that at our worst, we might not survive, but we are not without hope.

The midpoint of James's song cycle took us into the meaning of the lavender fields for James and his family. James and his family name "the lavender effect" as their collective choice, in the face of death, to live each day as a gift being given, not a possession being taken away:

We go to the lavender fields in early July.
Bright bristles paint the field with light violet vibrancy,
Each bud dripping with colour and fragrance,
Bristling with life, dancing with bees in the warm wind.
We say, let's not think about September,
When the greyed buds will crumble, tired and faded,
Littering tiny flower bits about like crumbs,
Let's not wait for the lifeless, desiccated sweet release
    of the petals,
Shaken from their stems and gathered up into sachets,
Their fragrance hauntingly strong as memories.
They say you have sixty months, maybe.
Days slowly unwinding, swirling away.
In early July the lavender blooms, full of life,
Its perfume all freshness, cleanliness, bright and calm.
We go to the lavender fields in early July.

The concert bore witness to what this lavender effect might look like. A group of exceptionally talented musicians partnered with James to bring his music to life. His family joined with him in overseeing every detail of the evening. And family and friends and music-lovers and poets and artists filled the hall and received this offering that was true, raw, hard, and beautiful. In the midst of cancer cells crowding into his body, James extravagantly poured out the costly perfume of his life. The sweet perfume of that offering filled the room and spilled out into the world.

We Didn't Choose This

Cheryl and Tanya would not have chosen to have their sister, Missy, die. They are two of the most compassionate and thoughtful people you could meet because of how they were blessed by her life and shaped by her death. The pain and difficulty through which Cheryl and Tanya have lived could make you question God, and yet the truth is that knowing Cheryl and Tanya is to feel like you know something undeniable about how God's love works.

Caitlyn has come to the brink of death constantly over the course of her short life because of the pain of living with borderline personality disorder (BPD). And she has also come to see how the intense sensitivity of living with BPD has allowed her to access a compassion for others, a righteous and energized anger at systemic injustice, and a hard-won courage from having survived her relentless desire to end her own life; these excruciating experiences have made possible their own beautiful offering.

James would not have chosen to die young of cancer. And also, the creative outpouring he offered in shaping his story into the *Lavender Fields* song cycle will continue for many years to help others navigate their own pain, fragility, and loss onto a path that nonetheless affirms life and hope in the midst of sickness and death. The lavender effect names exactly that possibility that our lives can partner with God in staring down the dark and dead reality of the tomb with the "wresting of life."

Author Parker Palmer notes that when the human heart breaks, it can either break into shards that create more hurt and pain, or it can break open, making possible new ways of sheltering and caring for one another. I would claim that because of

God's Spirit, even hearts that at first might shatter into shards can eventually find the grace to break open into new expressions of care and faith. And in fact, the living, breathing truth is this: the church has been, and continues to be, built "on the blood of the martyrs"—on lives who insisted God's power and purpose would not stop working in them, even in suffering, even in death.

We don't have some appealing but ultimately hollow promise of how our choices, our purchases, our lifestyles, our mental and physical fitness can make us into the best version of ourselves. We have instead, in the person of Jesus, a story that lays bare the suffering of lives that can and do fall apart anyway. We have the witnesses who show us where to look for light in the fractured places of our lives.

Set Free

Revive is a program created by the amazing Dawn Davis, published by Forward Movement, which we have been offering at St. George's for several years now. It is offered as a gift to our various leaders in the church, inviting them to take this time of learning and fellowship to nurture their relationship with God.

One of the first activities of our opening Revive retreat is to create a spiritual timeline. We map out our lives in ten-year chunks. We note our major life events onto that timeline. And then we consider where in those major life events we felt close to or far away from God.

Caitlyn participated in our Revive spiritual leadership program in the fall of 2020. Caitlyn chose to color code her spiritual timeline, using a warm orange to indicate the times that she felt closest to God. The warmest and most orange part of her timeline was in her early twenties when she described herself as an atheist and her working life led her to have to accompany a teenaged girl as she died from cancer. Although Caitlyn didn't believe in God, and although this young girl tragically did die, Caitlyn color coded this section of her life as orange because this girl's faith was so strong that she radiated God's loving care through the process of dying. A number of years later, Caitlyn would choose St.

George's to be her church. Caitlyn wrestles with God with such bristling honesty that she can't help but offer continual insight out of her own life into the presence and activity of God. She writes prolifically on the piercing and often bruised and bruising places where God is and isn't showing up in her life. Caitlyn references that teenaged girl dying of cancer as a powerful seed of faith planted in her own life.

In doing my timeline mapping with our first Revive cohort, I noticed something quite extraordinary. I noticed that there were several times in my life that I had gotten myself into a very dark place, when I was engaged in behaviors that were destructive to myself and to others. I did not want to end my destructive behaviors. I certainly didn't know how. And frankly, my behavior was entirely driven by a deep-seated conviction that I wasn't good enough and that I had to fix myself. "Always do your best" was the mantra driving my action and inaction.

I experienced the hand of God reaching through this whole mess of circumstances—some of my own making, some the result of the toxic messages we all unwittingly absorb from the world around us—that had imprisoned me. When I was a complete mess, God showed up for me—Jesus, in fact, showed up for me—and offered me a love that I hadn't believed in, asked for, or thought myself worthy of. When this happened, I experienced a wild freedom as a burden was lifted and a prison door was suddenly unlocked.

Healing from an eating disorder was one of several times that I can say I dramatically experienced this kind of grace. Interestingly, what followed was something very literally new. I was ordained as a minister of the church.

Jesus is so often touted as that great role model, the "What would Jesus do?" slogan offered as the only road sign needed in all of the crossroads of our lives toward our making the right, righteous, faithful, and true decisions. That's why "Always do your best" was on the front of that church sign. Jesus must make us better. But where I have viscerally encountered Jesus as something more than a role model from the dusty pages of history or a nice, tame idea is in the times I have been lost, stuck, willfully off track.

All of those years ago, I started to be haunted by a sense of calling to the priesthood almost immediately on the heels of falling in love with Jesus. I felt that telling catch in the back of my throat when I encountered his story and when it became clear to me that his story had something to do with mine. In Jesus, I began to suspect that my strivings and my failings and my personal emptiness all mattered, mattered consequentially and sacrificially and infinitely, to God.

God was reaching out to me in love, and even though I couldn't see how to solve the emptiness or how to be enough, there was a hand that was committed to clasping mine and never letting go, and there was the gift of life that was offered even though I would have never dared to ask.

DISCUSSION QUESTIONS

1. Why is it important to have an alternative to "always do your best"? Why is it important to have honest space and a message of hope in the times that are the worst?

2. Who are the martyrs in your life? The people whose witness reminds you of that hope amid life's greatest difficulties?

3. How has your life been shaped by the difficult circumstances not of your choosing? Do you connect with the stories of Cheryl and Tanya and James and Caitlyn, of how they didn't choose what happened to them and yet they were able to offer something beautiful and life-giving out of those places of suffering?

CHAPTER 15

God Is Not Indifferent to Our Sin

Leonard Cohen is almost as famous for telling us, "There's a crack in everything; that's how the light gets in" as he is for singing "Hallelujah." His words are another way of saying that the flaws are kind of the point. In being so accepting of our human flaws, though, we risk downplaying the seriousness of evil as well as God's opposition to those harmful impulses that can so easily distort our lives.

Relatively early into my ministry, I met a young man. He might have been five years younger than me at the time—late twenties. I will call him John. He showed up in my office on a Tuesday night just before we were to begin a new study. His eyes were bloodshot and darted like a caged animal as he explained he was newly converted to Christianity and was in desperate need of a church. He looked hunted, although at the time I assumed that he was stoned. I invited him to join the study that night, which he did gratefully. He had insightful contributions, and then I didn't see him again for a number of months. This time he showed up on a Sunday morning. He looked extremely serious but not like something was chasing him. His eyes were clear, and he scheduled a time with me later in the week.

Over tea at one of the local cafes, he told me a harrowing story unlike anything I had heard. John had been an atheist. He was a person of obvious intelligence. And, as would be evident in our later interactions, and which he himself would admit, John was arrogant. He wasn't content to simply hold his own beliefs about the nonexistence of God. He sought out opportunities to challenge Christians in what he took to be their delusions.

John eventually met a debating foe he wasn't expecting. He got into a series of intense conversations with a pastor who was versed in apologetics and who convinced John of the verifiable logic of the Christian faith as well as the reliability of the scriptures. John started to feel his rigid atheistic belief teetering.

One night, John went over to a friend's house, a Christian woman his age. He admitted to her that he was on the verge of accepting the Christian faith. The woman reacted in a way that John (or I, as the listener) would have not expected. A deep and frightening voice came out of his friend—a violent reaction to his conversion. The woman became possessed with superhuman strength and beat him up. He told me that his face was bruised and bloodied by her attack. Afterward, they both interpreted her actions as a moment of demonic possession. There were evil forces at work around John's conversion, and they had to have their answer.

Our Demons

I had never heard a firsthand experience like this one, but I believed John for several reasons. Many of us feel comfortable believing in God's goodness, in the Spirit of God working in our midst in beautiful and life-giving ways. But humanity's capacity for evil is well documented and so are spiritual realities that are harmful, destructive, and toxic.

In his book *Shake Hands with the Devil*, Roméo Dallaire describes his time leading the UN peacekeeping mission in Rwanda during the country's genocide. In the opening of the book he notes that people ask him how he could be a person of faith after seeing the senseless violence and murder that left so many thousands of people slaughtered. His answer is powerful: "I know there is a God because in Rwanda I shook hands with the devil. I have seen him, I have smelled him and I have touched him. I know the devil exists and therefore I know there is a God."[1]

I shared Dallaire's words at one of our Tuesday night studies, with John in attendance. He reacted viscerally. What Dallaire

---

1 Roméo Dallaire with Major Brent Beardsley, *Shake Hands with the Devil: The Failure of Humanity in Rwanda* (Toronto: Vintage Canada, 2003), xviii.

named in this book resonated with John's experience. Nobody is claiming that there is a horned guy dressed in red running around the earth with a pitchfork, luring people into the fires of hell, but the experience of personal forces of evil working against the power of God's love is real. John's experience is unlike any I have experienced. His experience is also in keeping with the fullness of Christian teaching. Jesus clearly understood himself as being in conflict with the forces of evil, casting out demons and demonstrating the power of God's goodness and love over and against the powers that hurt and imprison, ostracize, and kill.

I also believed John because the more I got to know him, the more I experienced him as a person who was undeniably locked in a battle. I think most of us, if we're being honest, know what it is to struggle with demons. We have our favorite seductions—the vices, the choices, the thought patterns, the pitfalls—that trip us up over and over again. They take different enough forms that we don't necessarily recognize them each time they snare us, and therefore they have enormous power in our lives to diminish us and harm us, as well as to lead us to bring harm to others.

With John, this battle was more explicit and explosive. He was baptized in our church at the Easter Vigil. He showed enormous promise for connecting with our young people, for teaching the faith, for using his razor-sharp intellect to inspire and open new ways of seeing God's power at work. He had an intense interest in biblical study, and although he was not a biblical literalist, he had a capacity for unpacking the relevancy and reliability of the scriptures. He was willing to help and serve in any aspect of the church's life that was needed. His great passion was to equip people in their faith, to enable them to be able to describe their own faith with such clarity that they could in turn instill faith in others, particularly nonbelievers. It is understandable that he would feel such a passion for this, given that he had been converted by a talented apologist; John believed that being a Christian was the greatest gift of his life. I and others in the church were grateful to have John offer leadership.

One Sunday, a number of months after John's baptism, he didn't show up for the morning service. That night I got a curt email saying that he was dropping every leadership role he had taken on, and we wouldn't see him again. It took many more months for him to tell me what had happened. It was one of a series of intense difficulties that I faced in church leadership all at once that felt like devastating setbacks at a time when the church had been flourishing. I had to work through some of my own demons in the fallout.

What eventually emerged in several hurtful emails was that John couldn't continue to live and serve in a church full of such half-hearted Christians. His intensity of faith and the sharpness of his intellect were great gifts from God; he showed enormous potential in Christian leadership. And he was tormented by his passion and intellectual prowess. His fervent belief became a stumbling block. He could not understand or accept the faith of those around him because it didn't manifest itself with the same verbal clarity he had, so he took it to be less heartfelt.

Perhaps John found a community of believers that was a better match. The problem is that "wherever you go, there you are." I suspect this particular demon continues to trip John up, unless he's found the grace to unmask it for the stumbling block it is and to be set free from the obstacle it will continue to present. John isn't going to be happy in a Christian community by finding the right kind of believers that measure up to his believing standards. He'll be happy in Christian community when this particular demon is disarmed.

I wasn't there when John's friend's voice transformed and she violently attacked him. It is an astonishing report. But I saw the other ways, the subtler and more insidious ways, that John's faith was attacked and undermined by forces that, whatever you want to call them, were working against his becoming the faith leader he could have been.

Believe or Bust

"Is there a hell?" It's a question that I get asked a lot as a priest, usually in quiet and worried conversations. It's rarely asked without there being a feeling that the stakes are personal. People are concerned about their own particular sins and whether those are a ticket to the wrong side of the afterlife.

This is one of the most unfortunate distortions of the Christian faith, which is that God uses a system of rewards and punishments—mostly centered on whether a person goes to heaven or hell after death—in order to wrangle human beings into the correct forms of belief and right living. We are to believe as a sort of eternal insurance policy, aligning our lives with the set of beliefs that we have been talked into assuming are the right ones in order to guarantee something good, rather than bad, at the end of our lives. Fear is the driving force in this kind of faith manipulation.

It is exactly this kind of rhetoric that has led many Christians to turn away from any discussion of hell whatsoever. We have been so turned off by the hellfire and brimstone message that has threatened people across the ages into toeing the line of faith that we have simply abandoned talk of hell, sin, evil, and most certainly the devil entirely. We have adopted a blanket universalist understanding of our faith. God doesn't punish people at the end of their mortal journey. The gates of heaven are wide open, and we're all welcomed in. We preach now to humanity's fundamental goodness and certainly to God's love for us.

A number of years ago, I was part of a conversation around baptism with some of my fellow priests. Several of my more senior colleagues were suggesting that the entire baptismal rite be rewritten: "The language is archaic. It doesn't make any sense in today's context."

The baptismal rite does begin with language that is radically at odds with our more typical mainline offering. The baptismal candidate, or the godparents speaking on the candidate's behalf, is asked to renounce all that corrupts or draws us from God's love: Satan, the spiritual forces of wickedness, the evil powers of this world, and our own sinful desires.

Layered into these opening questions are all of the ways in which this language and the teachings on which this language is based have been abused. Not only has fear been a driving force in hemming people into the pen of faith, but also demonic forces have been used to describe mental and physical illnesses that have been much better served by medical developments and an unmasking of superstition and stigma. They have also been used to allay personal responsibility in our own lives as well as to point fingers at, describe, and label the behavior of others. We can do much better in our teachings than relying on the crutches of hell, the devil, and the "spiritual forces of wickedness" that rebel, corrupt, and destroy.

It is appealingly simple to say there is no hell. God doesn't force us into belief by threatening us with the fires of eternal judgment. God's love overcomes all. The gates of heaven are open wide.

Except . . .

The problem with this simple answer is that it doesn't seem to be true. Hell is a widely misused teaching and concept. Hell is not God's threat of punishment, meant to be used to keep us on the right path. Instead, hell describes the truth of humanity's capacity for evil—a capacity that appears to be unique to us across all of God's creation. Hell describes our free will. We aren't forced into loving God. Freedom is essential in a relationship of love. Why set up a world in which we get to choose, where we can love and serve God (or not), only to press override at our deaths and corral us all through the gates of heaven, whether we want it or not?

Jesus referenced hell as the burning garbage heaps outside of the towns in which he was teaching. He used imagery that people could understand to describe a reality that most of us—again, if we're being honest—know in some capacity. We know what it is to be trapped, we know what it is to be cut off from God, consumed with the sort of burning garbage that Jesus described that can torment our souls and prevent us from knowing and receiving God's love. We know the fires of hell. We know them right here and right now. We know what it is to be tripped up and caught up in those desires, actions, thought patterns, and choices that draw us from God's love. We know the hurt of separation from the ways of love and life. We know that some of what leads us into hell is our own choices. And some of what traps us in hell are the hurts and harms we have absorbed from the people, circumstances, and world around us. We know this separation from God is real. We know the pain and destruction of that separation is real too.

God speaks into the suffering and dying of our lives. God speaks into the evil reality, the hell, of life too. God speaks because God is not indifferent to our sin, to our wrong choices, to the ways in which we get lost and hurt, to the separation that we can willfully choose.

Paul Bernardo and the Shadow over Our City

A shadow hangs over St. Catharines, the city where my family and I live. The shadow lingers in the background in ways that are often hard to articulate but that everyone who has lived here long enough would find hard to deny.

In the early 1990s, killers lived among us: Paul Bernardo and Karla Homolka. They were an attractive blond couple, married in our church, and surrounded by all of the trappings of beauty, youth, and middle-class respectability we find so reassuring. Hiding in plain sight, they stalked, raped, abducted, and killed teenaged girls for sexual pleasure. Among their victims was Karla's own sister.

My husband, Dan, sat at a desk behind another one of their victims, Kristen French, in their high school homeroom. He had a crush on this young, beautiful girl who may have inadvertently thwarted his dreams of asking her out on a date when she told him that she thought he would make a good priest. It was a Catholic school.

Kristen was abducted on Maundy Thursday on her walk home from school for the Easter long weekend and was never seen alive again.

As the story of her ordeal became public, Dan and his class-mates, Kristen's family, and the whole community wrestled with gruesome, heinous facts. It was a pivotal moment in Canadian history and one of the reasons why the easy freedom that we all enjoyed growing up—walking to and from school with a pack of friends but with no parental supervision, of spending long summer days and warm weekday nights playing in our neighbor-hoods with nobody particularly knowing where we were or when we would be home—is no longer. We couldn't grant our children that liberty today even if we wanted to. We would be reported for being irresponsible and unworthy parents. Instead, we arm our children with cell phones and texting plans, we put tracking apps on their devices, we insist that they communicate with us about where they are going and when they get there. We guard them with every option for safety that we can imagine. Because we know what could happen.

Dan was fifteen when Kristen went missing. He is a mid-dle-aged man now. And his dreams are still terrorized by the vision of what happened to her. He has had therapy. As a forty-plus-year-old, he still revisits and works through his trauma. He knows what can happen. He knows that evil is real, it has a face, and it can take away the things and the people that we love the most.

Down across the ages and throughout time, masses of people have found the promise of hell to be a reassuring one. They know how their lives can be utterly corrupted, distorted, and destroyed by those who wield their power without fear of any consequence for wiping out and beating down the poor and vulnerable who get in their way. They know the human capacity to find enjoy-ment and entertainment in the desecration of human life. They know that the most obscene, nauseating, debilitating, and vastly consequential atrocities can be committed by human beings and that in this life anyway, those human beings don't always answer for their actions in any real way. Their hope is in the fires of hell because they want to know that there will be a time when an answer is demanded and when justice is finally served.

Paul Bernardo is serving several life sentences in a jail in Kingston, about five hours up the 400-series highway from St. Catharines. Canadians expect he will never be released back into civilian life, although every couple of years he comes up for parole and his victims' families have to once again testify to how he has ruined their lives. Karla Homolka negotiated a much lighter sentence in return for testifying against her husband and was released almost two decades ago. She remarried, had children, and has mostly been living under the radar ever since.

Even the most tolerant and compassionate of Canadians of a certain age would tell you that they would gladly see these two people marched before a firing squad and shot. They might even be willing to pull the trigger themselves. It would seem that only the reign of God's terror and wrath would have the capacity to address the magnitude of the evil and devastation that they inflicted, for no reason other than their own perverted entertainment.

The Great Net of Heaven

A number of years ago, we had a sudden death in our parish. I will call him Terry. Terry was diagnosed as having bipolar disorder. He suffered from crippling depression. He was also kind-hearted, inquisitive, earnest, well read, insightful, and desperate for meaningful connection and authentic friendship in his life. I believe Terry would have liked to have had a girlfriend. When he died, his family repeated numerous times to me that Terry had died of natural causes—a problem with his heart. They asked that I name that specifically in my sermon at his funeral, which I did.

I got a call a few weeks later from a parishioner who asked why I had to say that Terry had died of natural causes. That isn't a common turn of phrase in funeral sermons. I explained that the family had requested it. I also theorized they may have done so because Terry had suffered from mental illness and from suicidal tendencies. Perhaps they were concerned if they didn't specify that people would think Terry took his own life. The parishioner explained that my statement had caused her some distress. My words had struck her as inauthentic, as if I were trying to participate in a cover-up with the family regarding the real circumstances of Terry's death.

Our conversation made me wonder at the reason for the family's request. Maybe Terry had ended his own life. And maybe they were ashamed for that truth to come out. Terry came from a traditional Christian background. It may be that they feared judgment on themselves and on Terry were the truth to be named. It may be that they feared God's judgment on Terry, for certainly it has been taught in the past by our Christian faith that to take one's own life is an unforgivable sin. Those who were known to have completed suicide were, at one time, prevented from having a Christian burial in consecrated grounds. It may be that they worried that our church would refuse to bury Terry if the truth got out. Whatever happened (and I confess to being haunted by not knowing), my parishioner had a word to say about Terry that seemed truer to me than the cloudy circumstances of his death: "I would like to think that if Terry did, indeed, come to that point of not being able to continue, and that he took his own life, that we could honor where he was in that place and trust in God's love there too."

This is the fundamental gospel truth. This is the banquet that was described by the prophet Isaiah and that Jesus used as a foundational image for his own ministry. Jesus kept gathering the lost sheep, the unforgiven, the ostracized, the lost, the lonely, the cut off, and the thrown out; he kept gathering them around God's table and feeding them, and feeding them again, inviting them to taste and see, to sit and stay, to hear their name called, and to take their place at God's table. The prophet Isaiah describes a mountaintop picnic that overflows with flavor and joy, that lifts the shroud of death and wipes every tear away.

Hell is real. Terry knew the realness of hell, whether he took his own life or not. He was at times marred by a pain that was all-consuming. And that pain may have led him, as U2 sings, to get "stuck in a moment that you can't get out of." My parishioner was right. As Christians we should absolutely be able to name and honor that truth because we also know a more powerful truth—the truth of God's persistent and faithful love. That's why we say in our creeds that Jesus spent those intervening hours between the cross and resurrection vanquishing hell. That's one of the central points of Good Friday and Easter Sunday: God claiming us from the darkness that we can't see our way through. If Terry died in the hell of an all-consuming pain that he himself couldn't see his way through, then we can trust that this is not the final word on Terry's life. Being in hell is a lived truth, but it doesn't mean that God leaves us stuck there.

I don't have to believe in hell. I know it's true. I know that we can get stuck there for all kinds of reasons, some of our own making, some as the collateral damage of living as fragile creatures in a broken world. I know that we can choose hell and that God honors that choice. And I place my hope in the God who fights for us, who goes out looking for the lost sheep, who sees through the crap of how distorted our lives can become through the lenses of fear and pain, and who never loses track of our true identity as God's beloved and never stops inviting us back to take our place at the table. As theologian Hans Urs von Balthasar notes, we don't have to believe in universal salvation. We don't have to believe that every one of God's children will make it through the wide open gates of heaven. But we can hope that it will be so.

In Marilynne Robinson's beautiful book *Housekeeping*, the narrator imagines a great net of heaven sweeping over her own isolated community of Fingerbone, plumbing the dark, cold depths of Fingerbone's lake to gather up all those who were tragically lost in its depths—including the narrator's own mother, who drove her car off a cliff to her intentional death for reasons of inner torment unknown to any but her. She imagines "a general reclaiming of fallen buttons and misplaced spectacles, of neighbors and kin, till time and error and accident were undone, and the world became comprehensible and whole."

There is, the writer suspects, "a law of completion—that everything must finally be made comprehensible." And she wonders, "what are all these fragments for, if not to be knit up finally?"[2]

Horrible forces are loose in our world that God addresses with justice and truth and condemnation, not with a sweeping blanket of niceties and unconditional regard. "I'm okay, you're okay, we're all okay" isn't actually a reasonable conclusion for God to draw at the end of all time for anyone who has experienced the rotting filth of what human life can be.

Does grace extend to Bernardo and Homolka? Does that law of completion and that general reclaiming that Robinson describes extend to those who commit the most appalling and senseless of atrocities against their fellow human beings? I have no idea. I find Hans Urs von Balthasar a reasonable authority on the topic. He doesn't know that we all make it to heaven. He isn't prepared to subscribe to that universalist bottom line that insists we all get saved. But he tells us that as Christians we can hope.

Evil Cannot Be Hidden

That hope can be a hard and ugly thing.

So much of what isn't working in our lives was unearthed and brought to light during the pandemic. Maybe it's because with the pause button on, we had time to think and consider in ways that we hadn't before. Maybe it's because the stress of COVID meant that our capacity to tolerate baked-in systemic injustice got maxed out.

In Canada in the summer of 2021, thousands of unmarked graves came to be identified on the grounds of the residential schools to which Indigenous children were sent, forcefully taken from their homes and families. It is expected that similar sites will be identified across the United States in the coming years too. We can't call them "discoveries" because Indigenous people have been telling us for generations that their children were taken and did not come home to them. The fact of these deaths has been known

---

2 Marilynne Robinson, *Housekeeping* (New York: Harper Perennial, 1980), 92.

all along. Yet Canadians found themselves suddenly undone by the voices of these lost children. We had known that they were ripped from their homes and the arms of their loved ones with the express purpose of "solving a problem." We had been aware of the inexcusable and awful abuse that went on in those homes, the inhumane living conditions, their names, their language, their hair, their clothing, and their families mercilessly cut away from them. But then there were the bodies, dumped in the ground. It is the complete lack of dignity and care that was afforded them, even in death, that brought us face to face with an evil that was enabled and empowered in every corner of our land.

"These were baptized children," National Indigenous Archbishop Mark MacDonald shared in a meeting shortly after the graves began to make Canadian headlines. "Even the theology of the church, even the basic understanding of our faith, that baptism makes us one in Christ, even that wasn't enough to make these children human enough for the church people who ran these schools to see them deserving of a Christian burial." Their bodies were disposed of, not on consecrated ground, not within the dignity and care of the prayers of the church, but rather thrown out as the gone, the forgotten, the never-existed. Thrown out like they weren't someone's child. Like they weren't a child that should have been loved and protected and honored by all of us.

Archbishop Mark also spoke of resurrection: "The power of Christ's resurrection is now speaking prophetically through these children to show us that this was a genocide. Children were herded by RCMP into places where they were decimated by plagues and poverty and hunger and abuse. The residue of this genocide is now being seen in these graves and calling attention to what happened. Evil cannot be hidden. Our task now is to listen."

The power of Christ's resurrection sometimes works on a time scale that is agonizing and horrific. It should not have taken until now for us to hear how a whole people were targeted and killed off and thrown away. It shouldn't have taken us until now to see the power of God's love in these children. It shouldn't have taken us until now to hear and treasure their voices.

This is the hard and ugly hope to which I subscribe: the undeserved kindness in God's relentless, and at times terrifying, faithfulness. There is a kindness in God still not letting us off the hook—giving us another chance to hear, to understand, and to act.

DISCUSSION QUESTIONS

1. How have you experienced the church's messages about sin, evil, and hell? Has it been used to scare and intimidate? Has it been missing from the conversation entirely? How have you experienced the misuse of these teachings? Do you agree that there is something missing when we don't talk about these things at all?

2. "Hell is real." Do you agree that hell is something that we experientially know to be real?

3. Theologian Hans Urs von Balthasar says that we don't know everyone makes it to heaven. But we can hope. Does this connect for you? Why or why not?

4. Why is it important to believe that "God is not indifferent to our sin?" What does that mean?

CHAPTER 16

Does God Answer Prayer?

We Can Ask God for What We Want

I sat with a faithful family on a warm summer's evening laughing about the seeming fickleness of God. James was my age, and he was dying of cancer. He had a wicked sense of humor and a boundless but never sugarcoated love for God.

Janine, his wife, describes her relationship with God as a gift that has been given to her. She once questioned an Easter sermon in which I had suggested that if the women hadn't shown up to the tomb on that first day of resurrection the world would have never known anything of the risen Jesus. God will meet us there, I had said, but we have to show up. Janine argued that I had downplayed, to a troubling extent, the activity of God. She experienced her own faith life as pure grace, pure gift, not something she attained for herself by will and by action, but a gift of love that has blessed her whole life through.

Laughter was a regularly dosed medicine in James's and Janine's house and had been part of how they had been dealing with James's incurable cancer diagnosis for the previous two years. Now, Janine's laughter had an edge to it. James's cancer had gone to his brain. Not only was he dying, he was losing his mind. If that wasn't enough, their house had decided to fall apart that one heartbreaking week too, with a basement flood being the most recent plague that the universe had visited on them.

I sat at their table listening to James describe his own sense of his disappearing dying self and to Janine's heartbroken grief that she not only had to lose her husband, but had to lose him while he was still physically with her. I felt some shame and guilt as I listened. The year prior, I had counseled Janine to pray about her fear that James might lose his mind in the process of dying. She had been racked with sadness that her husband was going to die. Within that sadness was the fear that he would die without the pieces of himself that she treasured so much. Her fear was prescient.

"We can ask God for whatever we want," I had told her then. "God wants to know our minds and hearts. Lay your prayer before God. Ask God to spare you that." I hoped that maybe she wouldn't remember my saying that, but of course she did.

"I prayed specifically for this not to happen," she said, sitting at their kitchen table. "Every bad thing that I have asked God not to happen through this has happened. I mean, is this God's sense of humor? I'm afraid to pray for anything now because then it just seems to allow the worst of the worst to happen!"

My shame and guilt at such obviously bad counsel turned to an angry disappointment with God. God may be the author of life, but sometimes I want to snatch the pen out of the divine hand and write a more cohesive narrative. I spoke those words of comfort to Janine with utter confidence. I told her that she could lay her heart bare before God, and I said it with the conviction that God would not let her down. I knew that the road ahead was going to be desperately hard, but I believed God would shelter her and show up for her at least in response to her heart's deepest and truest desire.

I stuttered out some of the words that I tend to say in such circumstances, words about how God doesn't make these things happen and isn't doing bad things in order to test or hurt us, words about God's promise to redeem even the worst and most random circumstances. The words felt hollow at first, but then started to connect with the painful reality in front of me. I began to feel that "something" that Frederick Buechner describes as a "catch in the throat." The Gospel of Luke describes it as an experience of "our hearts burning within us." Into our heartbroken conversation came the inescapable sense that the living God had come among us.

Was It Because I Didn't Have Enough Faith?

My grandfather, whom my brother and I called "Bubba," asked a question similar to Janine's a few years before he died—imploring and searching. He had had so many health troubles over the years, including several brushes with death. When my grandmother suddenly got sick and died, nothing had prepared him for being the one left behind after a lifetime of partnership.

We had all prayed for Grandma Jean, their church and community had prayed for Grandma Jean, and she had died anyway. She did so with her jaw set, just as she had set her jaw throughout her life when something difficult had to be accepted. She was good at accepting and surrendering, which was useful because her life hadn't been easy. She had little chance for education, leaving school when the Depression made it impossible for young people, especially young girls, to continue in school. She was one of the most creative, artistic, and deep-thinking people I have known, with the driest of dry humor and a taste for the absurdity of life. That she never had the chance to explore her significant intellectual and artistic gifts, that those gifts mostly only got to be poured out on the little circle of the household she eventually created with my grandfather, and that she lived her life with him in a supporting role feels to my mind like it might have disappointed her. Although she never voiced this disappointment or a sense that opportunity had been snatched from her, I believe I saw it in that set of her jaw and in the wide-ranging, intellectually challenging books she passed my way to silently support me, her granddaughter, in imagining other horizons of brave and bold possibilities.

After her quiet and resigned death, one evening in his stifling little apartment, my grandfather asked, "We're told that we can ask for anything from God, that if we have enough faith, it can move mountains. So if your grandmother died anyway, was that because I didn't have enough faith?"

I had told my closest family members that I was going to be a priest, which is why he asked me. His tone of voice was mostly sad and searching, and also there was a touch of anger that was directed at me because I represented the belief system that had failed him. All I could do was communicate that the size of his faith couldn't possibly have had anything to do with why my grandmother died.

Not for the first, or for the last, time I found myself annoyed with the Bible. Surely we could have all done without the suggestion—inked onto the pages of holy Scripture—that prayer is like a takeout menu, with personal faith being the currency needed to then get what we want when we put in our order. "For truly I tell you, if you have faith the size of a mustard seed, you will say to this mountain, 'Move from here to there,' and it will move; and nothing will be impossible for you" (Matt. 17:20).

Nothing Too Trivial

Bubba and I are in good company. What faithful person hasn't prayed for God's protection or for certain outcomes? And yet, just like Bubba, it is easy for any of us to lose even the strongest faith when circumstances don't go the way we prayed.

Poet Christian Wiman reflects on his relationship with God, wondering what it means to have our lives guided and informed by prayer. Wiman sweeps beyond all the individual concerns that we might be tempted to think God should fix for us or advise, like finding a parking spot or, in his case, being cured of cancer. He claims connection to God as so far beyond one person's own desires and needs that all we can hope for is to submit our darkness and disappointment to that greater power, as Jesus did in the Garden of Gethsemane. But then Wiman circles back and claims those petty concerns as part of our relationship with God too: "And maybe, just maybe, it even means praying for a parking spot in the faith that there is no permutation of reality too minute or trivial for God to be altogether absent from it,"[1] he concludes.

I pray for parking spots and cures and sunny weather and other particular outcomes all the time. I am surprised at how often my little prayers are answered. But I have learned that it is the offering more than the result that is important. Jesus encouraged a radical, unfiltered intimacy with God. Being clear with God about what is really on our hearts and minds must be part of honoring, or even just growing into, this intimacy.

---

1   Christian Wiman, "I Will Love You in the Summertime," *The American Scholar* (February 29, 2016), https://theamericanscholar.org/i-will-love-you-in-the-summertime/.

I didn't know how to talk with Bubba that night about any of this—intimacy with God, why we pray, and what those confusing words of Scripture might have meant. I imagine this would not have been helpful to him anyway. He needed a place to voice his sense of failure, his experience of being failed. I was that place that night.

The Elusiveness of Jesus

The road to Emmaus story from the Gospel of Luke gives us that wonderful phrase: "Were not our hearts burning within us?" It is offered in hindsight, after the unsuspecting disciples had walked with the risen Jesus and not recognized him until they sat down to eat together.

Many will argue that when Adam and Eve ate from the forbidden tree, with the fruit of knowledge of good and evil, that it wasn't a fall at all. It was the beginning of a journey of love. Their eyes were both opened and closed. Their eyes were opened to understand their own mortality and their own freedom. Their eyes were closed to the God who walks beside us always and forever. If they wanted to know and love that God, they had to seek; they had a choice.

On that Emmaus road, the disciples were accompanied by their friend and Savior, and the only sign they had was the "burning of their hearts within them." It took an invitation to dinner and their joining with this stranger in blessing and breaking bread, for their eyes to be opened to the presence of Jesus. And just as soon as they saw him, he was gone. Jesus keeps showing up just in time to eat. But then he is just as likely to "eat and run."

The elusiveness of Jesus is an important aspect of the life of faith. It's what should keep us humble and open to the voices and experiences of others. None of us gets to keep Jesus in the kitchen, a sort of pet there for our own enjoyment if and when we feel like hanging out with him. The searching is never finished, the learning never over, and just when we think we have it all figured out, it slips away from us again.

There are reassuring versions of faith, which obviously my grandfather had absorbed. These versions of faith suggest our relationship with God can be boiled down to a formula. If you have enough of it, things will go according to what you yourself wish and hope for. And if things don't go that way, that is a call to beef up on your own belief.

What we can miss, though, is the call to be on the lookout for where and how God might be appearing, and disappearing, in ways that don't match up with our own expectations. God refuses to be pinned down, and the divine MO is really about surprising us in the strangest places, only to leave again.

The Peace That Passes All Understanding

I realize now that I had mistakenly bought into that version of faith when I assured Janine that she should pray to God about what she most needed in James's illness and death. One of the great things about being a parish priest is the way my faith gets strengthened by the faith of the people I get to hang out with. James and Janine were two of those people whose faith inspired and strengthened me. I guess I assumed that Janine's open and faithful heart would offer a prayer to God that God couldn't possibly refuse. That was a reassuring thought to me when we were talking in the early stages of James's illness—so reassuring that I forgot that's not how it works, no matter how open and faithful your heart is.

On that summer's evening at their kitchen table, James was telling us that his mind was slipping away, and Janine was remembering the prayer that she had put so faithfully before God that this was exactly what she didn't want to deal with, and she wanted to know why God wasn't showing up for them. Nonetheless, there was that "catch in the throat" and the "burning in my heart" that alerted me to God's presence even though I felt totally confused and disappointed by God in that moment. We began to talk about where each of us actually was seeing or feeling God, even though God was resolutely not acting in the way that any of us wanted.

Everyone around the table said the clearest way they experienced God in James's illness was in the love and support and concrete actions of care offered by the people around them. I am amazed how many times I land here: God in the flesh, God showing up and speaking up in the people I meet, the people I am blessed to have in my life. My goodness, we can get it so wrong with one another; we can be so broken and so disappointing. But the most powerful access we have to God is most certainly one another.

I noted a few other ways that I was experiencing God's presence. James's and Janine's kids were maturing before our eyes, expressing love and care and strength beyond their years. In their grief, their hearts responded with compassion and a desire to connect with one another. They spoke courageously that they would rather have James for longer and have it be difficult than for him to die quickly and easily and their time to be cut shorter.

I noted that James was at peace with himself. That would change in the days after our kitchen table exchange, as his reaction to his ever-changing cocktail of medication caused multiple psychotic breaks. And yet, what I saw in that moment at the kitchen table was the gift of God's peace, a peace that breaks in, that descends and envelops, so inexplicable when everything else seems to be going to hell in a handbasket, we experience it as something almost visible, a thick blanket of God's presence wrapping around us. As the turmoil in their lives kept escalating, I watched and waited for that peace.

Most of all, I saw God's presence in Janine. More specifically, I saw Jesus's presence. I saw the story and promise of the cross. Janine was suffering. She was losing her partner, bit by bit. The only real prayer I could make out in her in that moment was "My God, my God, why have you forsaken me?" She felt little other than forsaken. There was nothing about this that was according to her plan or what she wanted. And the reason why it was so painful was because she loved James so much. The costliness of that love was the holy of holies around their kitchen table that night.

Let Me

We talked a few days later by phone, after everything had gotten much, much harder. Janine said she prayed the question that can sometimes be all we have: "Why?" Given how God had not responded to her prayers to that point, she had begun to wonder whether she should pray at all and, if so, what she should ask for. She wanted desperately to fix their situation and the pressure of searching for that fix was like a heavy, anxious weight. This time, she heard God speak in the quiet of her own heart. "Let me figure this out," was the answer. She realized that she didn't need to fix anything or figure it all out. God was in charge, not Janine. Janine finally felt that blanket of peace.

Praying isn't wishing. We're not going to upset or turn God off with the prayers of our hearts. God isn't going to give us an answer in order to teach us a lesson or to test us or because we were foolish enough to ask for the wrong thing. God also isn't going to choose how to respond based on the size of our faith.

A few years after James's death, Janine shared with me, "I learned that I could love so much more than I ever knew I could, and I also learned that I could survive so much more than I ever thought I could. I thought I couldn't love James if he lost his mind and I could—I could love him in a new and deeper way."

God responded to Janine's prayer with love and assurance. Janine didn't have to figure out the right course for James's death or try to discern why God wasn't allowing that death to unfold the way we thought it should. God was going to receive Janine's petition as exactly the holy offering of love that it was. And God was going to keep showing up, reassuring and hidden, descending with peace and leaving us in mystery.

DISCUSSION QUESTIONS

1. How is praying different from wishing? What is the point of prayer, other than asking God for what we want?

2. Why might it be important to ask God for what we want?

3. Martha describes the calling cards of God as "a catch in the throat," "our hearts burning within us" or a "peace which passes understanding." How do you experience the presence of God? What signs help you to feel God's closeness and love?

CHAPTER 17

I Don't Trust God

The Signs Were Clear

Several years ago, I was cycling home from work when I was struck by inspiration: I knew with utter certainty that there was a teenager named Tim in my congregation who I needed to invite to run the PowerPoint in our worship services. He was only peripherally involved in the church, and I knew inviting him to serve in that capacity would be a perfect match of his gifts and our church's need.

I talked with him. He was excited to be asked. Everything was coming together exactly as I had expected. But after helping once or twice, Tim stopped showing up. Perhaps because he was embarrassed about not showing up, he also stopped responding to emails and phone calls. My great moment of clarity, which felt like inspiration from on high, took the church's relationship with Tim into a nosedive.

I wish I could share some full-circle moment when that long-ago conversation planted a seed that bore fruit many years later. In truth, I have no idea what happened to Tim and whether my asking him to be involved succeeded in anything other than making him feel awkward and guilty.

The early months of 2018 were some of the most intense, unsettling, and educational of my life. Our Church was electing a new bishop, and I had spent many sleepless nights in the fall of 2017 agonizing about whether I would allow my name to stand should I be nominated. With a couple of signs too personal to explain and the support of my family, I accepted the nomination.

I look back on the lead-up to the election, and I can admit a very difficult thing: I was convinced I was going to be elected bishop. Sharing this may cast me in an arrogant and conceited light, but I am willing to admit it anyway because my error is of profound spiritual importance. It wasn't that I thought I was the best candidate or the most highly regarded. It wasn't even wishful thinking; I was ambivalent about what outcome I desired and leaned on the side of not wanting it. The reason I thought I would be elected is because I have rarely ever been so certain of anything as I was of God wanting me to be on that ballot. It is all too easy to assume that if I know what God wants of me, then I also know where God is taking me and why.

Why Did She Stay with Him?

Not too long after this time of personal upset, Hannah Brown was selected to be the bachelorette on ABC's hit reality dating show. Hannah's front runner was an evangelical Christian named Luke Parker. Luke was the first to say, "I'm falling in love with you." He and Hannah had obvious physical chemistry, and Luke shared Hannah's love of Jesus. Hannah was the most vocal lead in the history of the show in terms of the central role her Christian faith played in her life. She was regularly seen leading her contestants in a time of prayer. She openly discussed, not only on the show but also in interviews to promote the show, her "love of the Lord." It was clear that both Hannah and Luke believed this could be a match made in heaven.

Luke was also quickly depicted as the villain of the season. Not only did the other contestants not like him, the season was peppered with footage of Luke's blatant lies, occasional bouts of violence, and intentional deceits. He was openly disrespectful of Hannah, using his own beliefs to infer shame and judgment on her and her actions.

Even more than watching *The Bachelor*, I love listening to recap podcasts, particularly those that spend copious amounts of time wondering about various contestants' motives and what their words and actions say not just about them, but about society's values and expectations around sex, gender identity, romance, love, and marriage. Podcasters of this ilk could not have possibly had more fun than they did with Hannah's season. They will still note it as the one that far and away had the biggest audience tuning in to their commentaries. As the season played out, the question everyone obsessed over was, "Why can't she see through this guy?"

There is at least one villain in each *Bachelor* season. The producers of the show may have a hand in keeping that villain on for a few extra weeks in order to milk the drama they provide and to once again secure a captive audience with their week-by-week cliffhangers, but never had a season's lead been so obviously enthralled with someone so seemingly horrible. Never had the lead been so willing to see past so many obvious character flaws for the sake of some misguided notion of love. Speculation about what Hannah saw in Luke became more fevered every week that Luke stayed on the show.

"He was her pick from the start," some guessed, "And she just couldn't let that go." Others wondered at whether Luke was part of a pattern of relationships for Hannah. "I'd like to know more about her ex-boyfriends," commentators mused. There was talk about her age (she was the youngest lead ever cast) and her lack of experience in dating, and Hannah herself spoke about her insecurities as bachelorette becoming a factor in why she was so willing to latch onto the person that was most willing to tell her the words of love she wanted to hear (when he wasn't undermining her).

I would have liked to have been a guest on one of those podcasts as they mulled over these theories, because I am convinced I know exactly why Hannah was so slow to see through her grave incompatibility with Luke. Likewise, I believe I know why Luke continued to hang on to hope for Hannah's heart, even though he was obviously just as miserable with her as she was with him. They each thought God had clearly aligned their paths and their fates in order to end up together. They were both people of faith. They were both actively reading the signs. And they both believed that all signs pointed to the other. They trusted that God had brought them together.

Trust Can Lead to Crisis

Whether we're talking about God's almighty hand at work in *The Bachelor*, in the PowerPoint ministry, or in the Episcopal ballot, what we see is dangerous, and yet exceedingly common, soul territory. It is arguably one of the central reasons why we find ourselves sometimes tumbling into critical crises of faith, not to mention why we might opt for a whole slew of relationships and situations that clearly aren't bringing anyone health or joy.

Religious people can be quick to name our spiritual quest as that of aligning ourselves more and more closely to the will of God. Often what we really expect when we do so, though, is for God to provide us with fairy tale outcomes: not necessarily happily-ever-after but at least narrative arcs that could be best-seller material. It is the times when miraculous recoveries happen, when life is spared, when soul mates meet, and when impressive pinnacles of success are reached that we most glowingly speak of God's glory made manifest.

We don't talk about God's guiding hand when death, disease, and failure appear to take the upper hand. More specifically, we tend to speak out loud of how we sensed and responded to God's plan for us only when outcomes would suggest that we had read the memo correctly: the person we were to talk with says yes, the word we were given to say changes a life for the better, the courageous next step we believe is asked of us leads to visible accomplishment, the person we think God has given to us to love loves us back.

At the opening of one of our staff meetings, we were considering one of Jesus's early healing stories from the Gospel of Mark. Jesus's discernment had taken him across the lake to the land of the Gerasenes to a graveyard encounter with a man so riddled with demons that he had to be held under lock and chain well outside the confines of town. We read this story as a triumph of his astonishing healing powers, noting this as one of the earliest recognitions of who Jesus is—with Jesus's name and relationship to God clearly identified by the evil spirits possessing this man—and we connected this story to Jesus's emerging calling for his message to take him beyond his own tribe to be a "light for all people."

And yet, the Gospel writer takes care to let some of the sloppy details of the encounter speak for themselves too: two thousand pigs died through the healing ordeal; the townspeople were angered and frightened by the event; and when the healed man wanted to follow Jesus, Jesus instead sent him back to the people who were far from pleased to have him return. Even in writing the account decades after the fact, the Gospel writer couldn't really give an explanation for the story's accompanying disarray. We never hear from that demoniac again, what happened to him, how or if his story and his healing came to serve the purposes of God. We also have no idea whether Jesus felt like his encounter with this man, who he obviously believed himself called to seek out, was successful. What is clear is that even as God did not conform to Jesus's expectations, Jesus nonetheless continued to respond to God's call.

Do I Really Trust God? Or Do I Just Trust God to Do What I Want?

I was talking a lot in 2018 about trusting God. This should have been a red flag. Mostly, talk of "trusting God" makes me nervous. It sounds like standard religious language, and yet it can all too easily be a cover for assuming that God agrees with me about what I think should be done. In the same way that we trust family or friends to honor commitments or behave in ways that are consistent and reliable, we expect God's promises to us to be predictable and transparent.

There are actually few verses as terrifying and true as Isaiah 55:8: "For my thoughts are not your thoughts, nor are your ways my ways, says the Lord." Isaiah names God's closeness and encourages us in our seeking of the one who does hold the arc of our lives in loving hands, who promises that the purposes of love and joy can be fulfilled through God's people. But nowhere does it suggest that God is beholden to check those purposes with us first or to show how the puzzle pieces might or might not fit together.

In fact, trusting God is nothing like the trust that we might put into the people whose motives we understand and whose actions we can predict. Trusting God is surrendering to the whirlwind, the silence, the stranger, the wilderness, the wandering, the cross. It is also about surrendering to a supreme mercy and a great love. How many times do I fall, once again, into that most obvious and seductive kind of idolatry: making God's purposes into the image of my own oh-so-limited understanding. God gathers me up again and again, cradles and heals me, and in a thousand different ways shows me that I am loved.

In doing so, God breaks open the false idol of even that trust so that I can learn what is actually more important—to allow God to be God; to keep listening for God's call; to be prepared for all of the loose ends and strange outcomes that listening and following might entail; to be okay with seeds that I believe I have been asked to sow not ever bearing fruit that I can see.

Maybe trust isn't the right word for how I relate to God, and surely it isn't the right word for how God relates to me. And yet, despite my limited understanding, my false idols, and my constantly trying to be the one to lead in this dance of faith, what God does continue to communicate to me through it all is that I'm worth sticking it out with and for.

That's enough for me to keep listening for that still small voice and believing that God is asking something of me. It's enough to leave the fairy tale endings—or not—to God.

The Beauty of the Storm, the Safety of the Shore

My wise and funny friend Aidan grew up in the Roman Catholic Church. They define as a Genderqueer nonbinary person. They loved the church and loved Jesus, and they eventually had to part ways with both because it was clear that they couldn't both openly serve in the Church and openly pursue a partnered, faithful relationship at the same time. They have tried to come back to the Church several times but have continued to be hurt by the messages they receive about themselves and their marriage.

Aidan told me one Lent they were rereading the Gospels, starting with John and working their way back. They said that, despite all of the ongoing hurt they felt in their relationship with the Church, they were able to read the Gospels in a new way. They were reading them without fear.

I asked Aidan to describe what they meant. They told me that they had, so often in the past, read the Bible as the text of a hostile enemy. They were constantly on guard, looking for the homophobic subtext, prepared to be ambushed by hurtful and alienating messages, assuming that those were loaded in the arsenal and ready to be fired. But somehow, this time they were able to read them with a different lens and with an important new field of knowledge.

"I can trust it," Aidan said. "Somehow I know Jesus to be trustworthy. I know he's on my side. And so I know that what the Bible has to offer will be of value, will help, will be for me."

Aidan had recently finished the storm scene in John's Gospel. The disciples were crossing the lake in their little boat when a wild storm came up. As usual, they were terrified. But then they saw Jesus coming toward them over the waves, and suddenly they were on shore. "It's like I got it," Aidan said. "Jesus is allowing them to see the beauty of the storm and receive the safety of the shore. We get to experience the danger of the natural world, the fear and the storms of life, and Jesus transforms it for us into something beautiful."

DISCUSSION QUESTIONS

1. "Often when we say we trust God, we are really saying that we trust God to do what we want." Does this sound like familiar soul territory to you?

2. Have you had instances when you have thought you were following God's will only to have things not turn out as you expected?

③ What does it look like to trust God to be God? To allow seeds to be planted in our lives and to realize we might not see them bear fruit? To not ever see how the puzzle pieces fit together or how loose ends are addressed?

④ How does Aidan's story resonate with you? How does their insight, that Jesus is trustworthy, allow us to engage the storms and the beauty of life?

CHAPTER 18

God Is Not Helpless among the Ruins

Sometimes Things Don't Work Out

It had been a long time since I had felt such doubt. I was in free fall—over a cliff, with no idea where the bottom might be or how hard I might hit.

My mother-in-law had died in the early hours of the day. She was sixty-seven, and we had come to believe, terrible diagnosis aside, that we had more time with her. Prayer was working; the tumors had been shrinking. Then, suddenly, she was gone. My husband had spent the previous night by her side, holding her and reassuring her as she let go and her fight came to an end. He then spent the day making those painful calls to tell her loved ones the news, including having to tell his grandmother that her only living child had died. He made funeral arrangements; he picked out flowers for her casket and clothes for her burial.

He did it by himself because I was on the other side of the country with the kids, a nineteen-hour drive away. We were so blindsided by her sudden turn that we had gone ahead with vacation plans, with Dan hoping to join us once his mother was stabilized. Instead, we were days apart at the time when we most needed to be close.

But the kick over the edge came after I fell into a heavy, sad sleep that night. Dan had decided to fly out to join us on Prince Edward Island. He spent the day doing all that needed to be done and was going to fly out that night, to the wide expanse of ocean and red sand coast, the salty sea air, and the four of us holding onto one another. I was to pick him up at the Charlottetown airport the following morning and we would drive back to Ontario together.

Instead, just after I drifted off, I got his frantic phone call saying he was stuck behind two enormous burning accidents on the highway and that there was no way he was going to make his flight. Our friend Cheryl had picked him up with a three-and-a-half-hour window to drive him the one-hour trip to the airport, and that extra-wide window for travel wasn't enough.

I called the airline to try to book something else. I called Dan back several times hoping that something had shifted on that highway and he was going to get through. He had to make it. As the time narrowed in on his plane's departure and the airline apologetically informed me that all flights for the weekend to the Island were booked, Dan was still stuck. A jarring stream of texts and emails and Facebook posts flooded my phone as friends, family, and church members heard of Helen's death and were praying for us. How could so much prayer be directed our way and yet Dan couldn't get the one thing he needed so much? We weren't trying to move a mountain. We weren't asking for his mother back. We just needed one car-sized window in the traffic to open.

My dad has a saying that he refers to often when it feels like life is falling apart: "Things have a habit of working out." It has served as a nudge back toward sanity when we have become consumed with worry. A lot of the things we fear don't ever come to pass, and when we look back on difficult circumstances, hindsight reveals a greater wisdom, a bigger force at work. But the saying is only a nudge; it isn't the full truth. The chaos and disappointment of that dark night felt all-consuming. Life does sometimes fall apart; things don't always work out.

The Shepherding Is Real

I want to go back to that time when I was struggling to decide whether to accept a nomination to be on the ballot for bishop in our church. That experience shaped my understanding of what trust means in our relationship with God. It also offered me an insight into my experience of how God shows up for us. It's an insight I continue to return to.

There is a saying that God has a million Plan As, so choose Plan A. It is a nod to God's sweeping power, power that does not rely on micromanaging us into some foreordained outcome, but is alive and responsive to the random events and the free choices of our lives. Nothing in heaven or on earth—no missteps, no wrong moves—can separate us from God's love. If Jesus was willing to pass through the gate of hell itself to release the lost and imprisoned, then surely God can stay close to us through any variety of flawed and limited choices we might make.

This must be true. It is also true, in my life anyway, that God occasionally shows up as a relentless nag with a very particular agenda. I picture God as the now-deceased collie Cassie who belonged to my aunt and uncle and used to nip the ankles of her family members (especially Uncle Paul) as soon as we got out of bed in the morning, trying to herd us into the places she thought we should go.

Or, in especially sleepless nights, God is like my high school best friend, Mendi, who, when invited for a sleepover, chatted relentlessly well past lights-out. I used to watch the hours of the night slip away, my practical mind becoming increasingly frantic about how tired I knew I was going to be.

I had rehearsed the reasons why I was going to say no to a nomination in this election. My kids were still young at the time. My work at St. George's by no means felt complete. My fellow leader at St. George's, Scott, joked, "Your training is not yet complete, young Padawan." The *Star Wars* reference felt like the perfect answer to why I wasn't going on that ballot.

And yet, through a series of conversations with a wide-ranging and surprising cross-section of people (including my family), one or two signs that made sense only to me, and two weeks of heart-pounding, agonizing prayer and reflection in the middle of the night (hence, God as the chatty sleepover friend), I concluded that God was indeed asking me to be on the ballot. As with other such key junctures of discernment, it wasn't so much that I said yes to God; it was more that I gave in and stopped fighting.

As I was still waffling, Psalm 23 came across my path. I had been praying the psalms in the evening, trying to linger over words I have said and heard too many times to count. Psalm 23 was the next one up. I had never given it any real thought. It's not that I didn't like it. It has been too enshrined in stained glass, Hallmark cards, and golden oldie hymns for me ever to consider if I like it. On that night of indecision, however, it felt like I was reading the words for the first time. What I found was astonishing:

> God is the one setting the path.
> The path will go through some dark and dead places.
> Water will be provided when I am thirsty.
> I will not just be okay; I will be blessed.

I did not hear a promise for the future, for what God will do. I also didn't hear a choice given to me, a choice to allow God's guiding hand to lead me forward. Instead, I heard a description of how my life actually was. I heard the promise of the ultrareal.

I thought of all the times that I have had one agenda and have been herded into God's agenda instead and how blessed I have been by God's agenda. I thought of the dead-ends I have encountered, obstacles too great to overcome, commitments too many and too heavy to be able to juggle adequately, and I thought of the way through that God has always shown me. I thought of the times Dan and I have leaped together into the unknown after agonizing about the impossibility of being able to find a life that could possibly work, only to receive grace upon grace upon grace.

I realized as each word of Psalm 23 hit me that I didn't have to choose to believe God would be with me. God is my shepherd. That is not belief. It is experience. I would have had to expend a great deal of effort and talked myself through some complicated mental and spiritual gymnastics to decide that I was in it alone. Something had been asked of me, and in the end, I didn't even have to say yes. I just had to not turn away from the staff I could clearly see guiding me.

God Is There Anyway

God the Shepherd showed up that summer night when I was stuck on Prince Edward Island and Dan was missing his flight. God showed up in a way that was smaller and less dramatic than the highway opening I prayed for. It caught my breath despite that smallness. I was falling, and then someone other than me pulled the parachute open. I was cushioned. The prayers flooding in didn't prevent Dan from missing his flight, but they did provide a sudden peace, a deep and unarticulated sense of being in God's hands, even though I had just questioned God's very existence.

As my spiritual director Kevin commented, "We might not believe, we might not see, and amazingly, God is there anyway."

Eric Liddell, the famous Olympian whose life and faith was depicted in the movie *Chariots of Fire*, wrote, "Circumstances may appear to wreck our lives and God's plans, but God is not helpless among the ruins." [1]

God doesn't leave us helpless either. God sets it up so that we live our faith in community, we seek God together. It matters that we pray for one another because sometimes we are too blinded, too disappointed, too brokenhearted to find strength ourselves. We can't always see and feel and trust God alone.

In the years since that night, I have been aware of another important tool God gives us in asking us to pattern our faith lives around gathering, around the communal act of worship and coming together to pray. Eucharist is the word we use for worship that centers around the meal and sacrifice of bread and wine, the promise that in sharing that bread and wine together, Jesus is revealed to be with us. But the word Eucharist simply means thanksgiving. Our worship is shaped by the practice of gratitude. Gratitude isn't about being polite or optimistic; gratitude is about naming and claiming the fullness of what is really happening. Our worship builds our gratitude muscles.

---

1 Eric Liddell, *The Disciplines of the Christian Life* (London: Society for Promoting Christian Knowledge, 1985), 121–22.

That night I was caught and cushioned by the gift of communal prayer, and in the days that followed, my eucharistic training allowed me to step back from disappointment, breathe when the wind was knocked out of me, and see the blessings that abounded, even within the pain and difficulty we faced.

Things don't always work out. This is truer than the family saying I grew up with. Things don't always work out. But there is grace. There were all kinds of happenings after my mother-in-law's death that didn't go according to plan, that seemed needlessly difficult in an already difficult time. I think of Janine and James's basement flooding at the same time James's mind was beginning to break apart. I think of all the times when it doesn't just rain, it pours.

And also, there are the points of grace—gifts from outside of ourselves that have lifted us, given us strength or peace or a surprising burst of humor. There have been prayers that haven't been answered that I can admit were perhaps better that they weren't; there have been prayers answered in ways that I wasn't expecting. I have had to lean far more than is comfortable on the faith and provision of others. And I have had to rely on those gratitude muscles that are built week in and week out through the ups and downs of our lives as we keep coming back to the rhythm of church life.

We haven't been exempted from doubt and loss. But we have been shepherded through.

Living Waters

Pikangikum came onto the world's radar for a reason no community would want. It is a remote fly-in Indigenous community in northern Ontario. For a time, it had the highest suicide rate per capita of anywhere in the world.

Pikangikum is vastly underresourced. There isn't enough housing for their growing population. For many years, there was no school. Food sustainability is a problem. Most homes don't have running water or indoor plumbing. Homes that have had outhouses have mostly had to adapt those outhouses to address the housing shortage. When the elders of the community were asked by a group of concerned Ontarians from the south how they could help address the problem of youth suicides, those elders pointed to the absence of all of these basic building blocks of life. The suicides, they noted, were directly connected to the lack of hope.

I came to be connected to Pikangikum indirectly. I asked a question that other people across our Church were also asking of the same person, National Indigenous Bishop Mark MacDonald: "What can we do?" We weren't a group. We were just a question. We were people who knew about the lack of water in Indigenous communities, and we wanted to know how we could make things better. In a country as richly resourced as Canada, it was outrageous to us—as it is to most Canadians when they find out about this inequity—that so many communities would be without water, that this inequity would be so stridently racialized.

That lack of water is connected not just to broken promises that have built our country, but to genocide. Canada as a whole participated in an intentional project to remove "the Indian" from this much-coveted land and make them, their culture, their language, their ways, and their occupation of the land that otherwise was named terra nulla (empty land) disappear. The trauma of broken treaties, stolen land, and the one hundred years over which Indigenous people were forcibly removed from their homes and subjected to horrific abuses in residential schools is still written across these communities. Lack of clean running water and escalating youth suicides are just a few of the most obvious ways in which there is no such thing as mere "sins of the past." We are always shaped by who we have been.

We went into that first meeting with Bishop Mark with a lot of uncertainty and a great amount of hope. We wanted to help, but we were aware of how it had not worked in the past when the white man came in and presented Indigenous peoples with all of the answers. "There are going to be setbacks," Bishop

Mark said that night. "You need to know that upfront. This isn't going to be a quick fix. The most important thing here will be faithfulness."

We have raised money; we have seen clean water go into homes in Pikangikum. We have seen the federal government start to step up in some small way mostly because they have been shamed by us into action. We have asked what our next steps in this work can be, how we can connect with other communities, do more advocacy, and see this work advance.

We have also talked too much and not listened enough. I, for one, have continued to be undone by the stories and the history that comes to light in Canada. I haven't heard and understood all that was taken and all that continues to be taken still. We have wept with the people of Pikangikum through continued youth suicides and a deadly house fire that claimed the lives of nine people one spring. We have hit roadblocks related to the inadequate power grid in Pikangikum and the loss of various partners we have needed for implementing work and plans there.

Bishop Mark spoke at one of our Clergy Day learning events, a few years after our Living Waters group, Pimatiziwin Nipi, had been formed. He spoke about the change that he has seen across Canada as the movement toward truth and reconciliation with Indigenous brothers and sisters has taken hold and as First Nations' voices have become a vital part of the leadership of our country. When he first began his work as National Indigenous Bishop, he would speak to audiences of ten or twelve people. Now he speaks to packed rooms. He is one of the most sought-after speakers in our Church.

I know this is at least in part because of his thoughtful, wise, humble, and Spirit-filled words. Mark is an extraordinary leader. But when he was asked what has made the difference, why there is so much more interest now in this conversation between Indigenous and non-Indigenous Canada, Bishop Mark's answer was simple and surprising: hope. He said, "I think that, within First Nations' communities, and across the whole country, people are seeing there is hope. And they are willing to be part of that."

We didn't bring that hope or generate that hope. And although we have tried in a small way to be faithful, our faithfulness is only a drop in the bucket. "My people are resilient and strong," Archdeacon Val Kerr shared in an interview we broadcast for the Church in 2021. Val is a longtime friend, an Anglican priest, and a strong Indigenous woman. "We have suffered and we have survived. And also we have this strength."

She shared stories of survivors of residential schools, stories so horrific about the abuse that was endured, that I would have trouble even naming them on this page. But she also said, "I don't share this to make people feel bad or to point fingers. I share this so we can be honest, so we can learn, and so we can move forward."

In the first letter of Peter, it is written, "Do not fear what they fear, and do not be intimidated, but in your hearts sanctify Christ as Lord. Always be ready to make your defense to anyone who demands from you an accounting for the hope that is in you" (1 Peter 3:14–15). This is an accounting of that hope. The hope isn't that a group of non-Indigenous Christians has raised some money for running water. It's not the running water that is exactly the hope either, although it hasn't escaped our attention that water is a sign of the life-giving Spirit of God. The hope is that in the ruined landscape of relationships here in Canada, relationships between Indigenous and non-Indigenous peoples in which the Christian faith was weaponized against a whole people in order to make them and their beliefs go away, the hope is that even here in the decimated relationships, God would continue to raise up voices that haven't given up on a way forward.

Here among the ruins, the gifts of honesty, forgiveness, and the hard and complicated road toward reconciliation could still be possible, desired, and in small glimmers here and there, visible.

DISCUSSION QUESTIONS

1 How do you connect with the image of God as shepherd? Where and how do you experience God's guidance at work in your life?

2 "Things have a habit of working out," is a refrain that Martha grew up with. What happens when things don't work out? Does that challenge your faith when life goes off the rails?

3 Martha identifies hope in experiencing God's presence through the prayer of the church and in the voices of people in our church who have refused to give up on seeking a way forward. Where do you experience hope? Where do you experience the presence and power of God among the ruins?

CHAPTER 19

God Doesn't Magically Show Up, but God Shows Up

Linda is our office manager at St. George's. She is a dear friend. She is a "work mother" to me and the other priests at our church. She loves our kids like they are her own. At the center of Linda's story is the loss of her son Christopher. He died when he was just two years old. To know Linda is to know that this is the kind of loss from which a person never recovers. There are specific times of year—Christopher's birthday, the anniversary of Christopher's death—that are especially hard, even forty years after losing him. But of course, the grief can bubble up at any time. It can bring her to her knees when it does.

When Christopher died, the church that Linda and her husband attended did not adequately care for them. For reasons that I don't understand, they told her that a funeral for Christopher in the church wasn't necessary or appropriate. Linda and Leon were faithful members of that church and were devastated by this response. It was an astonishing addition to the pain they were already navigating.

Linda's is the kind of loss and grief that nobody should have to suffer. It is the kind of loss and grief that does not have silver linings. It feels wrong to suggest in any way that good has come out of Christopher's death, because that would be dishonest. It would be trying to rationalize a tragedy that is irrational. This is pain that Linda carries in her heart always, and that pain can be crippling. It always will be.

What I see in Linda, though, is a choice and a grace that also exists in that pain. She keeps choosing love. I believe that the capacity to choose love in this kind of heartbreak can only come from God, the source of love. It doesn't make sense otherwise.

I see Linda open her heart wide for those of us blessed to be in her circle, and she does so with a fierce and determined sort of dedication. I see her put love into action, making clear not just in words but in deed that she is willing to go the extra mile to offer care and support when any of us are in need. I see Linda hold other people up in their times of grief, carrying and responding to their explosive sorrow in a way that creates a safe place when someone else is so broken by loss that they also have been brought to their knees. I see Linda plugging back into the life of prayer, back into the life of the church—again and again. Not because her prayer has guarded her from the worst sorts of sorrow; not because the church has never failed her. She keeps plugging back in because she knows she needs to. She can't do anything, she can't keep going, except as one who is carried in the arms of Love.

There are no explanations for the loss of Christopher. There is nothing that can make this pain smaller or more manageable. And also, God is here.

They Saw Something

In the Bible, Thomas the disciple became famous for doubting his friends' account of seeing the resurrected Jesus. He insisted he couldn't believe in Jesus's resurrection unless he saw and touched Jesus himself. He was the one who spoke up for all his friends in expressing how difficult it was to believe this fantastical account of their dead teacher showing up for supper.

But when Jesus did show up, and Thomas had the chance to reach out and connect to the solid reality of Jesus's presence, he became the first to kneel before Jesus in an expression of radical belief: "My Lord, and my God!" Thomas's experience of the risen Jesus took him well beyond being able to believe his friends when they said that Jesus had been raised from the dead. Thomas was able to articulate what that meant and why it mattered: Jesus is the revelation and embodiment of the living God.

That invitation that Jesus issued with such love to Thomas—to receive, to accept the life and love that was right in front of his eyes—is before us too. The problem is that Thomas believed because he had access to confirming facts that we will never have. He was able to reach out and touch the resurrected Jesus. He was able to verify the claims of his friends, with physical evidence, that Jesus had risen. This is a great story, but what good does it do us, living in a time and place so far removed from Thomas? The risen Jesus doesn't show up at our supper table inviting us to reach out and put our hands into the dried blood of his three-day-old wounds.

And yet, Christianity spread like wildfire across the Roman Empire because of experience. Jesus showed up. For a few, Jesus showed up in a very literal way: a blinding vision and booming voice on the road to Damascus, like the apostle Paul experienced. For others, the experience was something else—and something no less powerful. They saw Jesus in the witness of Christians and then began to find access to that witness themselves. They could see this new truth made visible: "In Christ there is neither Jew nor Greek, male nor female, slave nor free" (Gal. 3:28). They saw an inexplicable courage in this renegade faith movement to be able to face death knowing that it wasn't going to have the last word, and they began to experience the truth themselves of how "neither death nor life, nor anything else in all creation will be able to separate us from the love of God in Christ Jesus our Lord" (Rom. 8:38–39).

They knew fear and anxiety and small-mindedness and division and even hatred and how all of these things can rule our human hearts and can become lord of even our most pious and well-intentioned communities. But they also saw the real and surprising power of forgiveness, of renewal, of new life, of reconciliation, of light in the darkness having its way across these dull and dying human lives, and they could see that, amazingly, this is more powerful than even the most ironclad empirical rule.

This Is Acceptance

In the language of ultrarealism, this is the place of acceptance. In the ultrareal church, we need to attend to this place where God shows up, where the risen Jesus is real and revealed in us. It's a place of faith, and it's a place that is based in the flesh-and-blood experience of how and where God's light and love so clearly shines in the midst of death, suffering, evil, and disappointment.

I could tell you about Mary Jayne's lung transplant, how modern medicine gave her the miracle of a new life, of her describing the process of dying, of her breath being taken from her so slowly and so methodically that in the last few weeks before her surgery, she had no fear, no sadness, no connection to the world around her at all. All she could think about moment to moment was drawing her next breath. Mary Jayne woke up from that surgery with lungs that could suck in the oxygen her body so desperately needed and with a visceral experience of rebirth.

I could tell you of two-year-old Grayson, who needed a heart transplant and who was dying every day in front of us, and when he was called for a new heart, how Dan gathered our church community in a time of prayer and Eucharist as I sat with the family for the hours it would take for the medical team to do the surgery, how he came out and his skin was pink for the first time, not the blue it had been since he was born.

There is the extraordinary story of Cheryl, who was hit by a car at the age of eleven, who was going to "either die or be in a permanent coma," and who regained full consciousness, reporting to her overjoyed family that her uncle had sent her back to them.

And there's the story of a faithful woman in Orillia, whose husband died, and hours later, while waiting for the funeral home to take the body, that dead man suddenly awoke and spoke, "God is good. God is love. It's all true. Tell everyone!" before dying again.

There are the countless people who have sat in my office and described their near-death experiences or their inexplicable encounters with departed loved ones, affirming that there is life beyond death and that God's relationship with us is indeed founded in love.

Occasionally, I have heard described, by people whose inner eye is better trained than mine, how God's calling card can be seen: when Lindsey's mother died, Lindsey saw a bright warm light come out of her body; when my uncle died, my cousin Becky saw our dead grandparents waiting at the window.

There are the stories, too, that aren't about modern medical miracles or coming back from the dead, but are simply the reports of uncommon sense leading people to act in ways that made outcomes possible that were life-changing: the mother who knew the doctors were wrong when they told her the baby had died in her womb, the parents who insisted on taking their child for further tests, the person who chose a different route to work and ended up assisting in an emergency.

I get to hear these spine-tingling, awe-inspiring stories all the time, of God's inexplicable activity on the move in our lives. But these aren't the stories that best reveal the power of God to me. God's power isn't best revealed to me in those rare moments when something inexplicable happens that interrupts death and illness, although I join with the whole community of faith in giving joyful thanks for when they do. And they do happen.

Rather, it's the stories of how Ryan saw the bigger truth of the life of the church while helping someone in their drug-induced stupor; James writing his music as he was dying; Janine's faithful and costly love as she stood by James's side, praying to God every step of the way; Caitlyn articulating and embodying God's love at work in her life even as her life has not gone as she would have wished; Aidan and Lorenzo claiming the trustworthiness of Jesus even as they have each been so harmed by the messages of the church. It's Danah falling into a relationship with Jesus even in the absence of the certain answers she was seeking. It's Bob on the dock with Jesus, and there is room for his sin and his saintliness. It's Linda, whose loss is bigger than anyone should have to bear and whose grief never goes away, and somehow, she finds, insists upon, receives, turns to the God of love. She does this in ways that concretely bless others.

Leonard Cohen's song "Hallelujah" has been so overused that, even though I'm a huge Cohen fan, I cringe when I hear another rendition of it on the radio. Cohen himself said that there should be a moratorium on the song. On the surface, it feels as if the song has been widely misappropriated. It is steeped in biblical imagery and a hard-won faith, and yet it is blithely trotted out in all kinds of the most secular of circumstances—from the opening ceremonies of the Olympic Games to various online fundraisers supporting any number of causes. I suspect it is so widely misused because it touches this deep and real place in our lives. It's the "broken and the holy" of who we really are. It's the sin, the failure, the falling apart, the ego that gets in the way, the blindness of stumbling through this life. And it's the lifting up of the presence of God in and through it all. Hallelujah means "praise the Lord." It's that hallelujah, that praise and that witness, in Ryan, James and Janine, Caitlyn, Aidan and Lorenzo, Danah, Bob and Linda, and so many others, where the love of God shines and blesses against all odds.

Not Just Acceptance

The thing about the Bible is that it's full of tragedy, of people who mess up and are messed up and are anything but heroic; it is full of strange and sloppy circumstances, of life going way off the rails—not just for individual people or families, but for whole communities. And there's death too. A lot of it. Nobody gets out alive. Even Jesus, who rises from the grave and is visibly taken back to God, had to physically experience what it was to have his breath slowly stolen from his lungs and for his heart to eventually stop. Each of the people who tell me their extraordinary stories also will eventually be felled by death. They have been blessed, but they won't escape suffering.

That's the thing about the church too. It's riddled with tragedy, death and dying, sin and failure. Death occurs and desperate diagnoses are delivered all the time, and people bravely, or sometimes with tears and fear, face the gravest of difficulties. Evil can be on the loose in our world and wreak havoc in our lives. Prayers don't get answered the way we anticipate or hope, and trusting God rarely involves predictable results or fairy tale outcomes. God doesn't magically show up to get everything back on track. But God does show up.

These stories—not of miracle, but of grace against all odds— don't just allow me to accept the life of faith and the gathered community that goes with it, they nudge me into the realm of being able to embrace the whole thing—lock, stock, and barrel.

DISCUSSION QUESTIONS

1. Have you witnessed stories of miracle that have inspired your faith?

2. Have you witnessed stories like Linda's that have also inspired your faith? Of people choosing love in the midst of senseless tragedy?

3. "The ultrareal of the church is where God shows up in the flesh-and-blood experiences of people's lives." How do you resonate with this definition of the church? How might it change our understanding of the church, what we value and prioritize, if we put this understanding of the community of faith at the center: "the church is the real people in whom God has shown up and been at work"?

4

The Gathered Church: Embracing Who We Really Are

CHAPTER 20

Change Is the Constant

In the middle of 2018, I took a sabbatical to work on polishing up my manuscript for my first published book. I also signed up for two half-marathons and a thirty-kilometer race. I had run halfs before, but the 30k was a new distance for me. It felt like the perfect sabbatical challenge, and I threw myself into training with gusto. It was easy for me to fit in the long training runs and to build up my weekly mileage. One of my running friends, Dianne, passed along her back issues of a variety of running magazines, and I pored over them for training and nutrition tips. I got to travel a fair amount over the course of my three months off, so I put in my miles on the red dirt roads of Prince Edward Island, the long flat trail by the South Saskatchewan River, and gazing around at the ocean and mountains of the West Coast. I celebrated various mileage milestones accordingly: chowder and French fries in PEI, an assortment of tacos with Jen at a downtown restaurant in Saskatoon, Catherine's fabulous seafood fettucine in Victoria, and homemade cherry pie made by Jeff's daughter Danielle to encourage us after a particularly hot and grueling run in Orillia.

While it was easy to find the time for running during those months, and it was fun to mark the training with these cross-Canada meals, it was also a time of chronic pain. The pain made sense. I was training for a new distance. No pain, no gain—it's a mantra we know well.

It started with plantar fasciitis in my right foot, which wasn't debilitating. I would wake up in the morning and have to hold back a howl hobbling my way to the bathroom on a foot that felt like it must be broken. But then I could run on that same injury with little to no pain. Nonetheless, I explored options for fixing the problem. I started doing foot exercises. I kept frozen limes in the freezer so I could roll my sore feet over them after a run, letting the ice and the hard, round surface work at the soft tissue of my foot. I went to see Beth, my awesome massage therapist, more frequently. She added to the suggestions for at-home therapy and strength-building exercises.

Then I began to wear supports in my various shoes. I have high arches, and it seemed from what I had read that just a little bit of arch support in my shoes, my running shoes especially, would help me heal. I started with these supports at the same time my mileage was in the final weeks of ramping up. I was running distances I had never run before. My feet felt like they were being properly supported, and that was encouraging, but man, did my legs and hips hurt. I consulted my running friends, who all affirmed the pain that came with pushing through to new distances. I upped my trips to see Beth. I even started stretching (my least favorite part of the running equation).

By the time I got to the West Coast for the final part of my sabbatical travels, I was staying with Catherine, and I was in my peak training week. Victoria could not have been a more beautiful place to run, and Catherine could not have been a more encouraging friend to cheer me through the challenge. On my last day in Victoria, Catherine went to work and I lined up my sports drinks, my podcasts, my energy gels, and everything else I needed for a 28-kilometer run, which would be my longest single distance ever, and it would be my longest distance before the race, now just three weeks away.

I was in pain when I started out, but it was pain that I was used to. I had mapped out a beautiful route through the city, circling back to Catherine's place twice to refuel. As I ran, the pain persisted, but it was dwarfed by the endorphins that began pumping through my body. I felt great mentally, the kilometers ticking by without any big, intimidating questions about whether I could do this. The temperature in the city was perfect. Forest fires were burning across British Columbia that summer, making the skies seem permanently overcast. But if the air quality was compromised, it didn't affect me. My breathing was steady and easy. The time on my final kilometer was my fastest of the morning.

The levels of pain shooting up through my right leg and into my hip were significant over the next few days, especially on the plane ride home. But again, that pain was overshadowed by the confidence and pride I felt in having accomplished this new distance. I took Tylenol and booked a visit to see Beth when I was back in St. Catharines, and I continued to walk around as much as I normally would, even if I was doing so with a limp.

I waited to feel better, but I didn't recover. I tried to run a short distance after a few days off, but my right leg wouldn't work. I was in pain constantly. A week went by, and there was no improvement. Beth worked at my leg but couldn't offer me any lasting relief. I was eventually referred to a sports chiropractor, Dr. Katie Pepper, who suspected a labral tear in my right hip. I saw her several times a week for months, during which time I was benched from running. I couldn't run my 30k race. All that beautiful time that I had devoted to training was soaked up analyzing what had gone wrong and how I was going to get better.

Accepting and Embracing—It's Complicated

Former archbishop of Canterbury, Rowan Williams, once noted in a speech about childhood development that "believing that change is possible—in yourself and in others" is a hallmark of being a mature adult. Although this particular lecture wasn't explicitly centered on our Christian faith, he drew on core principles of Christianity in order to offer a picture of what qualities we might want to model in our own adulthood if we are to then raise our children to adequately form them for the task of growing up.

Change is possible, in ourselves and others—this is one of the core principles of our faith. We believe in second and third chances. We believe in transformation and forgiveness. We believe in repentance. That means that although our lives are headed one way, it is always possible and sometimes necessary for us to turn around and go in a different direction instead. We don't believe in fate. We believe in free choice. We believe that we're not doomed to paths of destruction or bad karma. We believe in a God who interrupts our lives with grace.

There is a big risk to the ultrareal church, just as there is a big risk to ultrarealism in general. The risk for the church, and the risk for our own lives, is that we'll miss the nuance and opt instead for a clearer, crisper, and more certain black-and-white approach to living, which is always appealing. Magic bullet solutions are often more appealing than the hard and faithful work of prayer and discernment. But the fullness of life is not found in the black and white or the magic bullets.

The big risk to ultrarealism is that we give up our agency. If ultrarealism asks that we understand our circumstances for what they really are and then accept and embrace those circumstances, it is easy to conclude that what we're really doing is just learning to put up with the crap. The term ultrarealism comes from the realm of endurance sports, and man oh man, can there be a glorification of suffering in that realm. "No pain, no gain" can be destructive and even deadly words to live by. Similarly, there can be something remarkably defeatist, and even infantile, about, "I'm okay, you're okay, we're all okay." I'm only human, this is just the way things are, business as usual, you can't fight city hall: these are all easy cop-outs in the face of having to consider what Rowan Williams says instead—that change is possible, in myself and in others.

The big risk to the ultrareal church is that in embracing who we really are, we might walk away with the message that a whole lot of toxicity should just be tolerated, that change is not possible, necessary, or welcome.

What the Ultrareal Church Is Not

The ultrareal church is not an excuse for toxicity. It is not a caution against calling out bad behavior or any sort of permission to brush problems under the carpet. Sometimes people need to leave church communities, change church communities, or call church communities to account. Abusive, manipulative, and predatory people hide out in churches. Their behavior should not be sheltered or excused. The church has a terrible history of sheltering charismatic leaders of the church who exhibit toxic and abusive behavior because they seem to do so much good for spreading the gospel, because it feels like bringing their behavior out into the open also risks the possibility of calling the whole church into question.

To say that the people of God are sinful, that we are a mess, that we are flawed and fragile, that our flaws are "kind of the point" is not to say that bad behavior just needs to be accepted. To say that the church needs to get real about who we are instead of always focusing on who we wish we could be is not to say that we aren't also on a path of how we seek to be better, how we hold ourselves to account, how we look for and call out where change is needed. The ultrareal church does not look down its nose on those who need to leave or call out faith communities that are causing them harm. Ultrarealism in life is not about persevering at any cost.

I didn't know about ultrarealism back when I was training for that sabbatical 30k race. Looking back, I understand that if I had been able to embrace what was happening on that fateful Victoria run, when the endorphins and pain were both pumping through my body and I was inadvertently and seriously injuring myself, I would have known to stop. Embracing the reality of that situation would have been to respond to my body telling me that what I was doing was not working, that what I was doing was harming me. Embracing the reality of that situation would have allowed me to put aside my short-term goals and the schedule I had created for myself so I could figure out what I was doing wrong and stop damaging myself.

I beat myself up for a long time after that injury. I had a lot of time to beat myself up, as I drove to Fonthill for chiropractic sessions with Dr. Pepper, as I did my rehab exercises, as I hobbled instead of ran. I rehashed the warning signals I had ignored; I wondered if I would ever run again; I cursed myself for being so stupid.

But the injury also offered me a chance to embrace something. I injured myself because I didn't know better. And that's okay. I didn't know how to differentiate between the pain that was part of the process and the pain that was telling me to stop.

Injuries are part of the package as a runner because a runner has to learn about different kinds of pain; the only way to do that is by trial and error. This is the ultrareal of injury: I can't go back and change what happened, but I can learn going forward. The injury taught me things about pain and my body that I didn't know before.

That's ultrarealism in running: sometimes the right choice is to stop. Ultrarealism in life also must allow for the possibility that stopping is the right way of embracing a situation. Sometimes relationships need to end. Moves need to happen. Jobs need to change. How we understand our vocation needs to shift.

The Ultrareal of Change

I led a study at St. George's in 2017 to celebrate our 225th anniversary as a church community. I delved with the group into the beautifully written history of the parish, penned by retired bishop of Niagara, Walter Asbil. A few themes emerged in our exploration.

The boom times in St. George's and in the Anglican Church of Canada—the times when money was flowing, new parish churches were being erected in every neighborhood across North America and people were packing into our pews for four services a day, filling the church to overflowing—was also when the seeds of decline were already being sown. Those boom times were great, but they also helped create the marginalized church of today. Likewise, in the many ebbs in the ebbing and flowing of St. George's life, renewal and resurrection were bubbling under the surface of waters that appeared at the time to be stagnant and stuck.

Here is the other thing in our study. St. George's is known as a traditional, staid congregation. St. George's wasn't, as a whole, immediately welcoming of me as its first female lead priest coming in at the age of thirty-five and seeming to shake things up. "Too much change!" was the rallying cry that I heard for months after starting. What people were really reacting to wasn't all of the moving and shaking I was doing—I tried to be as careful as possible coming in to the tradition and legacy this community had already built for itself—they were reacting to me. I was the change.

But if our study revealed anything, it was that change has been constant. A 225-year bird's-eye view of the church's history made it clear that change is the most consistent part of who St. George's has been. A living, breathing organism is in a constant state of growing and declining, of dying and being born. We should be reassured that the church is no different. The change in the church reminds us that we are alive.

Ultrarealism, if we're not careful, can sound like a stance against change. Accept and embrace who we are. Stop wanting to be who we are not. Stop wishing we could be someone else. And yet, in running, sometimes the ultrareal response to the circumstances in front of us is to change course, to adapt and shift, to pick another plan, to walk instead of run, to go home via another route.

As a leader in the church, I am known as a change agent, not as someone just playing chaplain to the dying church that is. The last thing that the church needs right now, or that the church needs out of this book, is permission to give up. I want us to fight for a better future; I want to advocate for and lead the way in how women continue to be welcomed into the ranks of leadership—not as "small men," but as people whose unique experiences and perspectives shift who we are and how we go forward. I want to stand up for equal marriage and watch how our vision expands when previously marginalized voices are afforded dignity and previously shunned relationships are seen as blessed. I want to decolonize. I want to hear the voices of Indigenous siblings whose leadership can so transform us. I want to dismantle systemic racism. I want music of all sorts to be heard in the walls of our building. I want young leaders with new ideas to be raised up. I want to fearlessly open our doors and go out into the world. I want to rethink the structures of our church to better reflect the living, breathing reality of who we are.

That's the thing about ultrarealism that absolutely can't be missed. Ultrarealism attends to what is happening now, the circumstances we are really in, the reality of who we are, and it does this not just to accept what is in front of us, but also to react accordingly. In other words, part of ultrarealism assumes that change is constant. That's why we attend to what is, rather than what was or what might be. Because what is is fleeting and subject to change. Because what is requires our response.

The last step in ultrarealism is embracing who we are. And sometimes it is in embracing who we are that we know what we most need to do is to change.

To Embrace: Acceptance and Change

This book began with my feeling stuck and burned out. I was in good company in 2020, and many of my colleagues in ministry ended up opting for a change away from parish ministry. It took me some long months of prayer and discernment, along with heavy doses of wishing that an alternative to parish ministry might present itself, for me to end up staying. At that time in my life, the ultrareal of my situation wasn't just that I had nowhere else to go, it was also the grace of coming to realize—not without significant amounts of tears first—that where I was is also where I wanted to be. For others, the ultrareal of their situation was the recognition that the road they were on was no longer working.

The pandemic pressed the pause button on all of our lives and also became a catalyst for change. We might have felt like we were all going nowhere, and in fact, we were collectively considering in profound and transformational ways who we are, who we want to be, and what is and is not working. We were collectively forced into that great spiritual terrain of the wilderness. Our tradition has long seen wilderness times as essential to the growth and renewal of our relationship with God. Maybe it didn't always get framed as spiritual terrain, but the reflections that poured out of us during COVID—about the importance of community, about how interdependent we are and how we might better care for one another, about justice and equality and dismantling systemic injustice—these were all essentially spiritual questions.

That pause button led me first to real vocational distress and unhappiness, then to a semidisappointed resignation that I had nowhere else to go. I needed the help, companionship, wisdom, prayers, love, and support of others in order to get somewhere past resignation. I needed God's slow and quiet and collaborative healing to be at work in my life to be able to do more than sigh and stay. It wasn't immediate—it took time and a lot of fits and starts along the way—but the ultrareal of my vocation wasn't just to accept that I'm a priest and God is calling me to parish ministry. The ultrareal of my vocation was also that I have a choice.

That's the deal. God creates and fashions us. God leads us and calls us. There is a vision with which we are created. God gifts us and calls that vision forth. And we can say yes. That's Mary's great witness. She was a brave and faithful young girl who was asked to do this impossible thing. She was created to be the mother of God, to be asked by the angel to bear God's Son. She responded with her words of choice: "Let it be with me according to your word."

There's room for all of it, all the complexity, in living faithful lives. There is room for acceptance and change. There is room to be chosen and to choose. There is room to say no and to say yes. There is room to sigh; to say, "I guess . . ."; and then to embrace it after all and once again.

Stuck with Each Other and Choosing Each Other

An ongoing theme of this book has been that we're stuck with each other. That's a big part of the understanding and acceptance I offer us as the church. In order to see who we really are, we have to understand and accept that biologically, God sets up this life so that we are bound to one another. Spiritually, God does the same. We must figure out how to love one another and live with one another in order to love and live with God.

That's the ultrareal church. It's not that we can't do better, call to account, and seek change. It's not that toxic relationships, communities, and individuals simply need to be tolerated. It is, however, true that there is no real way of looking after ourselves

without also attending to our care for one another. It is also true
that our lives are built to learn the giving and receiving of love.
That means that to know joy and fulfillment, we have to figure
out how to be with one another. That's the stuck part. But there is
also a choice. It is true that we're stuck with one another. And it's
also true that we can choose one another. That brings us through
the understanding and acceptance of who we are as the church,
the body of Christ, the community of faith. But ultrarealism can
land us in a destructive and defeatist place if there isn't also this
step beyond just coming to terms with what is. The question
before us now has to do with that movement from the sigh of
resignation to the possibility of joy. What does it look like not just
to accept, but also embrace who we are?

What Do We Embrace? The Faith of the Squiggling Puppy

Our dog, Bruce, is seven pounds of sunshine and affection. He
likes to be carried downstairs in the morning for his first outside trip of the day. His dog brother, Dr. Pepper, usually sleeps
in the living room, and Bruce is filled with anticipation about
seeing Dr. Pepper and checking out the backyard with him. He
squiggles with excitement all the way downstairs. He squiggles
with the faith that there are arms there to hold him; he squiggles with the lived understanding that there is a support system
around him that will prevent him from squiggling right out of
my arms, falling down the stairs, and hurting himself. He squiggles knowing that he is loved and cared for.

Maybe this is a helpful place to locate our lives of faith. We
are a little like Bruce, the squiggling dog. We are figuring out the
world, our place in it, and what it all means, in the context of
being held in love. More than that, though, we are all part of providing those arms of love for all of our squiggling. In this last
section of the book we consider the ultrareal call to embrace—to
wrap our arms around this unfiltered mess of who we really are
and to choose it with love.

In these final chapters, we consider what we might be embracing. We are embracing the infected reality of being bodies in this world. We are embracing what it means to have no walls. We are embracing the story we share. We are embracing our prayer. We are embracing apocalypse—the crazy, uncommon sense of our lives—and the very real gift of being people who together can nudge the curtain, can invite one another to see, can help one another see better and more clearly the God who has come close.

We are embracing the truth of why we have been gathered and why we continue to choose that gathering. It is in these flawed and fractured arms that we can embrace one another, embrace the reality of who we are. It is in these flawed and fractured arms that we can also discover what it is to be embraced.

DISCUSSION QUESTIONS

1. Sometimes embracing the reality of a situation means leaving it. Can you think of instances in your life when this has been true for you?

2. Change is the constant of our lives and also the living, breathing reality of being the church. Where have you feared change in the church? Where have you experienced change as a blessing?

3. Why do you think that this final step of ultrarealism is so important? Why is our choice to embrace who we are, as people and as a church, so potentially life-giving?

CHAPTER 21

Embrace the Infection

> Our bodies are transitory vessels built from recycled carbon like every other living being on this planet. Bits and parts of you have probably been a cricket or a dinosaur or a single blade of grass on the prairies.
>
> *Eden Robinson, Son of a Trickster*

The Body Knows

I had a sore throat for roughly 60 percent of 2020, which means that I spent at least that amount of time fretting that I might have COVID. "I'm not sure anyone on the face of the planet has had more COVID tests than you," my friend Brian commented. To be fair, I only had three tests over the course of the whole year. When our kids returned to COVID-era school, though, the number of tests across our family added up. Any sniffle, any headache, any inexplicable coughing, and kids were being sent home from school and told not to come back until they had received a negative swab.

Brian was right, though. Two of those three COVID tests were the result of a mild hypochondria that I felt entirely encouraged to develop. It's not that the sore throat I had was imagined; it was a manifestation of the crazy-making times we were living in, when an obsessive focus on our body's aches and pains was suddenly part of how we were to show our care for one another. It was our job to worry that we might have the coronavirus, and I was taking that job seriously.

That mind–body connection can result in some skewed information at the best of times. I can think I'm hungry, when really I'm bored. I can feel exhausted, when actually I'm sad. I ran

28 kilometers on that injured hip and had no idea because the endorphins were pumping so hard that I didn't feel the pain.

And also, this mind–body connection can relay knowledge that is spot on. I know exactly the part of my stomach that feels like it has a ball of lead sitting in it when I am confronted with a word that God is asking me to hear when I would rather not. Shocking occurrences ripple through my body like a web of electricity. My breath catches in my throat in one particular spot when I am awake enough to realize I am in the presence of the holy.

In Paul's first letter to the Corinthians he asked the fledgling Christian community to remember that "your body is a temple of the Holy Spirit within you, which you have from God, and that you are not your own" (1 Cor. 6:19). Paul issues this reminder to his fellow Christians within a conversation that warns against adultery, fornication, drunkenness, and a number of other popular sins (popular in the sense of both how much people like to commit and condemn them), which is why this verse usually gets quoted as a threat. Don't swear, get tattoos, have the wrong kind of sex, or eat too much sugar, because doing so dishonors God.

What gets missed in that easy read are the radical promises of the gospel. We are promised that in our body we can share in Jesus's resurrection and be raised as he is. We are promised that in our body we are woven into the life of community, that our body is part of Christ's body. We are promised that God honors, blesses, draws near, and is revealed, incarnate, in our biological, flesh-and-blood reality.

This isn't just a promise, it's an invitation to knowledge. The body knows. Our living, breathing bodies, temples of the Holy Spirit, have information to impart, information that we ignore at our own peril. And also, that information needs to be filtered through the communal reality of how one body exists within our collective body, how the living God who comes close to me must be discerned and loved within the context of community.

This communal, relational body has been shouting knowledge at us for a long time. It's not just the rising sea levels, the extreme weather patterns, the escalating temperatures, and the wave of mass extinction through which we have currently been living that has been shouting. It's also that our rising rates of depression and mental illness, our collective obesity, and our need for an increasing variety of substances to numb and loosen us also have urgent messages to convey. In response to these various iterations of crisis, we have tended to double down on the questions of individual need and personal salvation—What do I need? Desire? What fulfills me? What inadequacies are holding me back? What can fill me and my void?—and what we have failed to hear in all of our relentless focus on weight, diet, exercise, mental and physical wellness is this similarly relentless calling back to the truth of who we really are.

I am not an individual. I am a relationship. Biologically, not to mention spiritually, I am intricately and intimately connected to the carbon, oxygen, water, and energy being recycled among all living beings. I, and several billion other I's, are all trying to live on this planet as if my body is just about me. Yet that core spiritual knowledge was offered to us so long ago, and we have continually failed to hear it: that body, that temple, isn't just about me; this body is part of a body; and in that body, God is at work. The body knows, but the body knows within the context of how my living, breathing cells connect me to the whole world around me. My anxious mind spent most of 2020 manifesting this physical symptom in my throat. I suspect that what my sore throat was trying to tell me wasn't that I had COVID, but rather this isn't just about me.

What Else Isn't Just About Me?

While negotiating this sore throat 60 percent of the time, we had this worship conundrum on our hands. The conundrum, for us at St. George's anyway, wasn't how we were going to lead worship when we couldn't be together in person. We were fortunate to have had a livestream worship ministry for years before COVID came knocking on our door. In mid-March of 2020, just after our churches shut down for in-person worship, the bishops of our Anglican churches in Ontario decreed a eucharistic fast. We were allowed to lead worship online for our people, but that worship needed to be something other than the sharing of bread and wine at communion.

To say the reactions to this were mixed is an understatement. There were those who were in complete agreement with their choice. Many others were outraged. Different communities in our denomination have different worship practices, and for some, this was like asking people to get a personality transplant: Who can we possibly be if we can't celebrate the Eucharist? For others, a different form of prayer and worship suited just fine.

I was ambivalent about the fast. I was upset on behalf of other colleagues who felt undermined by the dictum. But I myself didn't have any desire to celebrate the Eucharist without my community. I couldn't even honestly say that I had missed the Eucharist. In those early months of the pandemic, I was struggling with personal issues in terms of my relationship with the church. If pressed, I could have identified that I missed the whole package of the singing, hugging, laughing, weeping, worrying, discerning, imagining, giving, serving, praying congregation of people who show up week in and week out. I missed how in being together, in worship, we are better able to hear and receive God's response to the hopes and needs we offer up. I was not identifying the receiving of bread and wine as a separate component of loss from all of the other pieces of loss that were piling up at that time.

Which is why I was surprised to have this spiritual realization land on me like a ton of bricks one Sunday morning: we must start celebrating the Eucharist again in our communities. One minute, I was singing the alto part to one of my favorite hymns, and the next, I felt this revelation as a shockwave moving through my body. I could feel the absence of that thin wafer of bread on my tongue, that sip of too-sweet wine in my mouth as a desperate longing. I realized in that desperate longing that I had gotten something terribly wrong. A lot of us had it wrong. I hadn't been fussing about the eucharistic fast because I was treating it as an individual choice: something that is or is not essential for me, something that is or is not essential for the community I serve. I had been so caught up in my own drama that spring that I had not carefully thought through what was actually being lost in our worshipping lives.

We needed to do this because it is never just about the people who happen to be gathered and who receive bread and wine in that moment. The Eucharist can be understood as the family meal, the ultimate expression of the gathered community coming together to receive their true identity once again at God's hand: "the body of Christ." The Eucharist is, then, about the gathering of our people. And the Eucharist is, through the church, offered for the life of the world. It is the meeting of God's love with, the offering of Jesus's own life for, the broken state of affairs that is the world's life. It is a vehicle of God's reconciling activity across our earthly home. It's about the gathered community, yes, but God forbid that it remains just about the gathered community. God forbid that the prayers of the people who are able to show up on any given Sunday would be merely about us.

It became clear to me that I needed to celebrate the Eucharist because I was a priest and this was my vocation. It didn't matter whether I felt I needed it. When I looked at our aching, wheezing, anxious, physically divided world, with no clear path forward, I knew that my job was to lift that up. Even if we could not be together, we needed to invite God's healing power of love to meet us.

Surely those prayers have power, not just when we are all together and COVID precautions are over, but in the thick of lockdown living too—because God is powerful, and God promises to speak into all that we offer. God doesn't have a spiritual scorecard keeping tally of how many prayers are offered for any particular need before acting. And yet, surely we believe that prayer matters. Surely we believe our eucharistic prayer matters.

To say that it matters is also to say that there was a spiritual deficit, a cost, to having had all of our Anglican congregations suddenly halt our eucharistic offerings. Yes, we live into our identity as the body of Christ in so many ways, and I saw the kindness, compassion, generosity, and sacrificial service of the church flourish in the pandemic. But if we don't also claim the differ-ence made by the church's faithfulness to Jesus's call to "do this and remember me," we run the risk of falling into the social club, huddled-church trap of thinking that our witness goes no further than just our own little group.[1]

We also run the risk of thinking that only in an idealized set of circumstances can our church gather and worship meaningfully. Along with my longing for the bread and wine was the longing of all of us: to be together again in our beautiful sanctuary, with our beloved community, and with the whole place buzzing with excitement, favorite hymns, joy, and love, so grateful to see one another after this mandated time apart.

But of course, the church doesn't exist or worship in ideal cir-cumstances. The church has been most powerfully formed in hid-den back rooms in times of persecution, in defiant groups coming together in the middle of a field in the height of communist Europe, in war-torn countries when that bread and wine is lifted up as a life-line—a brave and resolute lifeline—in response to the destruction and shadows that otherwise seem to dominate. The church exists and gathers and worships in cultures that have deemed it irrelevant and when decline in the face of secularism has been named as inev-itable. It is a brave and defiant and beautiful thing to gather in that context too. It is also generous. It is generous because what we are doing is for those who don't think it matters too.

What we needed to find our way toward was the bravery and defiance and generosity being asked of us in this less-than-ideal moment.

Some Giggle; Others Weep

A picture in a March 2020 *Hello* magazine showed duchesses Meghan and Kate shaking gloveless hands with people lined up to greet them outside of the big Commonwealth Day church

---

1 Judy Paulsen, professor at Wycliffe College, talked about the characteris-tics of the huddled church at a Clergy and Licensed Lay Workers Educational Day for the Diocese of Niagara on May 21, 2020.

service. Unlike the other members of the royal family who were observing the suggested protocols of wearing gloves or engaging in touchless greetings, Meghan and Kate were as warm, close, and approachable as ever. They may not have said so themselves, but what they were doing was exemplifying a core Christian principle. Jesus used physical touch to offer healing: not just the physical healing of renewing the skin of lepers or restoring the sight of a man born blind, but also the healing of removing stigma, restoring people to relationship, reclaiming dignity, and combatting misinformation. Ever since, people of prominence—Princess Diana and Francis of Assisi would be two well-known examples—have been able to break down barriers and restore stigmatized people to the life of community by the offering of conspicuous touch.

Although Kate and Meghan's press was initially favorable, by the time their father-in-law, Prince Charles, was diagnosed with COVID-19 several weeks later (and much later we discovered that Prince William had also contracted the virus) it was abundantly clear that the duchesses had been wrong to have ignored the advice of health officials. Kate and Meghan were representative of a faith conundrum we all share. We are to model our lives on the Lord, who "kissed the lepers clean," who didn't shy away from the symptomatic and stigmatized.

Our worship is awkward. We expect people to sing together and at strange times; we act out ancient rituals that can seem, on the surface, incomprehensible; we join our voices together in prayers and creeds and confessions that assume an awful lot about all of these people actually being on the same page. We have moments of silence when everyone is left with the almost unheard-of task of dwelling in their own thoughts.

The most awkward worship service of the year, though, hands down, is Maundy Thursday. Maundy Thursday marks the final night of Jesus's human life before his arrest and death on Good Friday. We understand that on that final night, around that final meal, Jesus broke and shared a loaf of bread, and he passed around a cup of wine. He said, "When you do this, remember me." If that act of sharing bread and wine weren't uncomfortably intimate enough—everyone's hands grabbing onto the loaf of bread and wrenching off a piece to eat, everyone's lips and tongues and spit getting all over the cup of wine and into the cup too no doubt—after supper Jesus did something even more uncomfortable. He got on his knees and washed the feet of his disciples.

We know that at least Jesus's dear friend Peter was repulsed and horrified by Jesus's coming close to him in this unsavory way. So it is not surprising that it is also uncomfortable, unnerving, cringe-worthy, and for some, hilarious, when on Maundy Thursday each year, the church enters into Jesus's story through the ritual of foot washing. Parishioners come forward, take off their socks, and allow their priests to pour warm water on their ticklish, blistered, usually somewhat smelly care-worn feet and to then gently dry their skin with a towel. Some people giggle. Others weep. Emotions run close to the surface when we let someone touch us in that manner. It is strange, awkward, intimate, and beautiful.

In 2020, foot washing was not allowed because of COVID protocols. In 2021, it was still not allowed, but I found a way to get around it.

"I'll wash your feet," I told my husband, Dan. "Then you wash mine."

He was going to be joining our service that night anyway, and our being in the close proximity necessary to wash feet wasn't breaking any rules because of being from the same household.

"I'm not really comfortable with that," he balked.

"That's the point," I told him.

What Now?

For a long time, it was thought to be a particularly meaningful thing in small enough gatherings of the Christian community to have everyone congregate around the altar at the time of communion and to have each person pass the bread and wine to the person beside them. I participated in countless services like this, usually with a small and fresh loaf of bread instead of wafers. It was a slow and messy affair, each person chewing the chunk of bread while also trying to break off a piece to pass to the next person. That chunk of bread always felt impossibly huge when you were trying to get it swallowed before then turning to the next person with the words "the body of Christ," as you gave a chunk to them too. The chalice was easier to manage, although I would often notice with a shudder who in the circle did a lousy job of wiping the common cup before passing it along. Especially when we used real bread, by the end of the circle there would be at least a few crumbs floating in the leftover wine, and sometimes more.

It seems incredible to contemplate now how we could have so casually participated in such risky, illness-spreading behavior. And yet, for all of its awkwardness, it was considered by many to be an exceptionally emotional and holy experience. I would hazard a guess that this kind of eucharistic gathering is gone forever.

COVID has forever changed the way that we will physically connect with the germ-infested body parts of others. Online worship is here to stay, and many opt for that convenience and ease of gathering even when in-person is available again. What about masks and physical distancing? Vaccine passports and temperature checks at the door? Will we ever just casually shake a bunch of strangers' hands when we share the peace? How about hugs and the common cup? Will those things ever come back? How much of our COVID protocols are going to become part of business as usual?

This is a tremendous loss. The more careful, distanced, sterilized, and regimented our worship is, the less it feels like the physical, hands-on, "taste and see," and "touch and heal" ministry of Jesus. It is a loss, but it is also a gain. During COVID, we became aware of our microscopic, microbial interactions with one another as never before. We got in touch in a new way with a truth that Jesus was continually revealing: there is no such thing as self-sufficient, disconnected individual life. We couldn't be together because we are connected. Any decisions I made to protect, or not protect, myself had an impact on the whole world around me.

The thing is that this wasn't just true in COVID. It has always been true. My own well-being is dependent on everyone else in this great circle of life. That must be the takeaway for the church—for the church that had to find other ways to gather because it could not gather. For the church that invites people to gather again but that needs to make a case for why it matters. Everything has been put on the table, which means that everything is up for grabs. The church needs to make a case, even to the church, for why the community of faith should be essential to us going forward. In a world where we have become aware of just how infected with one another's life we really are, why lean into that truth? Why allow ourselves to be infected with one another?

This is the reality I would name and to which I want to give my all: that the gathered church is essential because it bears witness to the world the truth of who we really are. Whether or not an individual participates in a faith community, the inescapable truth for every creature on this planet is of our connectedness. The great crises of our modern-day living are all rooted in having lost sight of that truth. The gathered church bears witness to ourselves, and especially to the world, the inescapable truth of how our lives are finally and forever bound together.

Not Ideal, but Necessary

We had been collectively asked to hold out on the Eucharist until we could get it right. Instead, we had to figure out how to lift up our eucharistic prayer anyway. I hope that what we learned is that what we do is necessary, even if it's not ideal.

Especially if it's not ideal.

Our bishop lifted the eucharistic fast in the early summer of 2020, several months after it had begun. We were allowed to celebrate communion again, albeit online. We didn't know it at that time, but we were still a long way from any semblance of returning to "normal" patterns of worship. Our picture had to change. For a long time, for months and months and months, an inconceivable amount of time when lockdown was first declared, we couldn't be together physically. Instead, we had a skeleton crew and a livestream camera inviting our community to join in through nothing but adequate bandwidth and the power of the Holy Spirit.

I could say that I learned to trust that this would be enough during those strange months. But I didn't have to trust, I could experience. As soon as those words, "the grace of our Lord Jesus Christ, and the love of God, and the fellowship of the Holy Spirit," were uttered, it was never just our skeleton crew any longer. The little band of us in that sanctuary were connected, week in and week out, to the multitudes of people who couldn't be with us physically in that moment. That grief and loss became part of what we offered up to God, and in a very real way, we were together. The eucharistic prayer opened up into "all the company of heaven," the way that it does when we are in our sanctuaries full of people.

The broken and limping people were there too, the ones I know personally and the ones whose stories I can only imagine. God's response, "the gifts of God for the people of God," has never been offered merely for those of us physically present, in this, or any other moment. The taste of the kingdom in our mouths is the taste of union with all of the body, scattered and isolated.

DISCUSSION QUESTIONS

1. "The body knows." Martha discusses the message her sore throat was sending her during COVID, as well as other times that her body had wisdom and knowledge to impart to her. How do you resonate with this statement? What do you know in your body?

2. Martha notes the mistake that was made in thinking that the eucharistic prayer of the church is only offered for the gathered community. Do you think of our church's worship as being offered for more than just the people there? Why might it be important to shift our perspective to this wider understanding of what the gathered church is for?

③ "We are infected with one another. Every creature on this planet lives in relationship to the earth, air, water, and fellow creatures around them." This is a spiritual statement, but also a biological statement. Martha argues that this is the essential offering of the gathered church, to stand in witness to the world the truth of how our lives are bound to one another. Why is this witness important? How does this witness speak to the crises of our times?

CHAPTER 22

Embrace No Walls

All of Me

About twenty of us sat around a circle on the first Tuesday evening of our Anglicanism 101 class. We asked each person, "Why are you here?" "Pass" was a permitted answer. It was a varied group, including many longtime or even lifetime Anglicans taking the course as a sort of spiritual refresher, as well as a number of people new to St. George's and to our tradition.

Their answers reflected their diversity. Some had no particular draw toward "Anglican," but rather were looking for a community committed to living its faith through its care for others. Some people had never considered the question—being Anglican was just in their blood. Still others poignantly described journeys that had led them to feel that this might be a tradition in which they could be accepted for who they are.

Many of us teared up around the circle as Anita, a woman fairly new to the church at the time, said, "I was part of one church and felt like certain parts of me weren't accepted; I was part of another church and felt that other parts of me weren't accepted. I believe that all of me might be accepted here."

The Anglican Church has been traditionally known as both the big tent of faith, as well as the middle way. Its formation was solidified under the reign of Queen Elizabeth I of England, who had a vested interest in unifying her country by creating a church that could be tolerant enough to include a whole range of practices and beliefs, as long as those practices and beliefs weren't opposed to the interests of the country as a whole. The thing about a tent, as our former national Anglican archbishop Fred Hiltz once said in a sermon at St. George's, is that it provides shelter, but it has no walls.

I'm Not Sure Jesus Was Inclusive

It is standard practice for churches to proudly name ourselves as inclusive as an antidote to the poison of so much officially sanctioned hate. This seems right and good for many reasons. We want to challenge long-entrenched patterns of language that, for example, suggest God is an old white guy and Indigenous Peoples are mascots for our sports teams. It is important to offer gestures of welcome and hospitality to those who might otherwise be considered outsiders. There is value in our various institutions conscientiously seeking qualified employees who represent the diversity of our people and our stated belief that all genders are equal.

Jesus's ministry is said to be inclusive for very good reason: he was able to see beyond labels and appearances, his ministry of hospitality was central to his overall ministry, and his welcoming of sinners and outcasts was a critical piece of the controversy surrounding his execution. Jesus is for everybody—not just the people of a certain religion or skin color or ritual practice or who measure up to set purity codes. However, to label his ministry as merely inclusive is to miss the urgency of the choice that Jesus presents: "Repent for the kingdom of God has come near."

"I do not know you," Jesus, at a setting of final judgment, said to those who ignored the hungry, thirsty, and lonely in this life. "This is my command," he said on his final night—a command, not a suggestion—"that you love one another." To count ourselves as followers of Jesus, we are to obey that command. Jesus's ministry wasn't one of sweeping us all into the embrace of God. He threw down the gauntlet of ultimate human choice and freedom. When outsiders, ostracized from society, judged as contaminated and contaminating, were welcomed to the healing and reconciliation of the gospel, Jesus made no lukewarm generalization to gather them in to God's love. He laid claim to a burning insight into that individual's soul: "Your faith has made you well."

We take our inclusive Jesus and slap our ubiquitous "All Are Welcome" sign on the front of our church. Though I count myself lucky to serve and have served in churches that genuinely make an effort to welcome new people, I know how easily even welcoming churches can miss the mark. To call ourselves inclusive can function as a reminder to be constantly training our eyes and hearts to see and care for those to whom we might otherwise turn a blind eye, but the word can also suggest inertia, self-centeredness, and, if we're not careful, a dangerous self-righteousness.

Inclusive Can Be Destructive

I have never been hired by a church that didn't hope, or even expect, that part of my job would be to attract young people. I have been blessed to serve in churches and ministries where young people, young couples, young children started to respond to what we were doing and showed up in noticeable numbers.

Inevitably, a culture clash comes somewhere along the way. New people want to serve in the community and in worship, and they have different ideas about how things can and should be done. They offer sometimes surprising perspectives and specific needs in our Bible studies that can be unsettling. Children come into our space and into our worship, and they want to play the piano during announcements, wander up to hide behind the altar rail during communion, drip wax on the lovely carpets when they are asked to hold a candle, and generally disrupt the peace some people think is essential to good worship.

Congregations find themselves at a crossroads in this culture clash. How much is the established community willing to be changed by those who are just beginning to wonder if there is room for them? People are known to leave churches over this kind of culture clash. They wanted "young people" to come in to assure the survival of the thing that they love, but when the thing they love changes as a result, the fine print on this spirit of inclusion is more than was bargained for. This might not seem like a big deal. Yes, inclusion has its consequences. And, again, I count myself fortunate that although every church I have been in has come to this point of culture clash, we navigated those choppy waters in a way that allowed for the disruption of new life.

But there are demeaning and destructive dimensions to inclusion too. As a woman in ministry, I have run up against the condescending attitude that even four-plus decades of women's ordination in our tradition hasn't been able to eradicate: that we can join in this thing called the priesthood, but we better be as much like men as possible. Our bodies better not look too feminine, our leadership better not rock the boat, we better not have needs around maternity leaves and childcare. It has been far too easy for the most "successful" women in ministry to have been those who can slip most effortlessly into the male mold already established.

Even more horrifying is the relationship between inclusion and colonization. Colonization was driven by a spirit of inclusion, of bringing the whole wide world under the umbrella of empires that were thought to be evolved and enlightened. The residential school system took Indigenous children from their home under the guise of making room within white culture for them—as long as they became like us.

It's not that there aren't examples of inclusive agendas that have allowed people to join us as they are, dressed how they want, talking in the way that is most comfortable, bringing their culture and background with them. It's just that it is all too easy to miss explicitly articulating a reciprocity to the arrangement. We can be so intent on welcoming people in that we miss the part of the story where we get changed because of the newness they bring. It is an extremely common thing to tout our inclusion as a means of boosting our own ranks and assuring the survival of the thing we ourselves love.

The most dangerous thing about getting on our inclusive high horses, however, is this patronizing self-righteousness shrouded in the language of welcome and good intentions. It is all too easy to assume that "they" should need and want what we have; it is all too easy to come at a spirit of inclusion with a frame of mind that edits out difference with a blind and inadvertently pompous destructiveness.

Rather than figuring out how to make room for people in the setup we already have, perhaps what we need to attend to is how God pushes us out of our comfort zones and into the big, wide, wall-less world. Yes, there is a baked-in assumption to our faith that what we have received in our relationship with God needs to be shared. But that must be tempered with the urgent reminder that this sharing is less about getting people to join us in what we are doing and more about looking for how the voices of those who are not part of what we are doing will bless us with new wisdom, experience, and perspective.

Gathering and Sending

I was out hiking with my friend Catherine and a few of her friends. When people discover that I am a priest, they often have an urge to explain to me, without prompting, why they are not part of a religious community.

"This is my church," Catherine's friend said, waving her hands to indicate the majestic canopy of trees, the forest floor, the glimpse of blue sky beyond, and the streaming sunshine giving our surroundings the look of an enchanted and mysterious fairy tale land. Hers was one of the more common explanations I hear. People don't come to church because they feel closer to God when they're outside.

If I were to name how I feel closest to God, it would be through music: hearing a song throbbing with emotion, questions, praise, and storytelling, joining my voice with the voices of others. Occasionally, that happens for me in church buildings, but usually it happens outside of any explicitly religious space—like in the car during long road trips. I have no trouble appreciating that many people feel closer to God in places other than traditional sanctuaries. And it is not at all hard to imagine that one of the most natural places to feel this closeness would be in surroundings where the miracle and beauty of the world in which we live is so unmediated by human interference, where you feel as if you can glimpse the mind of God in the superfluous diversity and the intimate interconnectedness of the natural world.

I relate to what Catherine's friend shared, but it makes me sad—not because I believe that the person in question had chosen a lesser closeness. It makes me sad because somehow the church has failed to communicate who it is and what it offers, why it is an integral part of pursuing the richest possible relationship with God and the deepest fulfillment of my own soul.

This misunderstanding starts within the spirit of inclusivity. Inclusive language frames church as a place to go to pray and worship and draw near to God. It is welcoming, ideally, but you have to come there. The problem is if I can do all those things elsewhere, church feels redundant. But church is not a place to go. It is a community. And that community isn't located in a place ready to welcome you in. That community is like yeast kneaded into bread dough; that community is kneaded into every bit of our existence.

Jesus's inaugural act in his public ministry was to call disciples. When he made this Good News proclamation—"the kingdom of God has come near"—he was clear that it would be inseparable from the life of community. If we are not willing to be tethered to our neighbors, then we don't really know God. I don't go to church to find a place where I feel close to God. I become the church in order that my soul may be pushed outward from my own lost rabbit hole of self-concern into relationship with the people and places around me.

Which is why, although church isn't a place, it does help to go to a specific place repeatedly as part of what our church living includes. It helps to meet in one spot so that the doors of that spot can be opened to the stranger who will need to know where you are when they are looking for food or sanctuary or welcome or prayer. It helps to meet in one spot so that the church can then go out from there to care in very specific ways for the neighbors and neighborhoods outside of our doors, because caring for the people and places where we find ourselves is essential in opening our hearts to the love of God.

Wherever it meets, the church is built according to the pattern of Gathering and Sending. We are gathered out of our own individual bubbles into the life of community. Our own worries and heartbreaks are combined with the worries and heartbreaks of our neighbors, and together we pray for ourselves and our

world. Our ears are trained to hear in other voices a more complete picture of God's purpose and love, to see in new ways how
the world around us is teeming with the blessings and beauty of
God. Our souls together allow my soul to be more complete. This
soul can then be sent into the world, to all of the places where
God needs me to participate in how God will be made alive in the
relationships and conversations just waiting to happen, and also
to all of the places where God is most alive to me—like singing
along loudly to a favorite song in my car or walking under that
canopy of trees.

Generous and Expansive Language

We held an Advent Café sermon series a few years ago called
"Images of God." Fourteen different people, most of them not
ordained, offered a sermon reflecting on an image that they
found particularly meaningful in understanding their relationship with God. Celeste talked about God as Father. Liz picked
a small wooden cross that spoke to her sense of spirituality. Paul
saw God as the Gardener. Aidan connected to God through
the image of Mary, Wendy saw God as Wind, and Gary chose
the Scapegoat. The variety of images was rich, and sometimes,
depending on how you yourself had seen God, the images could
be unsettling. For those who wanted to break out of the lock-
box of seeing God as male, the image of the Father, for example, might have felt like the wrong sort of step. And for those
attached to our more frequently used words and pictures for
describing God, the variety felt challenging, which was okay.
The preachers in our sermon series shared a lot about their personal faith. People sheltered one another with respect and care.
Minds opened up. Everyone got something meaningful from
the experience.

I fully support the value of choosing alternatives to the male
imagery and pronouns we might use for God. Although I don't
know anybody who would say that they really believe God is a
guy, it is in becoming aware of the dominance of male language
we use to talk about the divine that our attention can be drawn

to the limitations we so freely and often impose on our imagination. Nothing gets people in our pews more irate than changing the words of one of their favorite hymns in order to open up the language. That ire is, in and of itself, a potentially valuable thing. We pay attention; we are disarmed and irritated by words that otherwise might slip around us like a warm bath. The possibility opens before us of recognizing that the same language that feels so comforting and poetic to one person can be deeply unsettling and upsetting to someone else.

Ideally, that recognition works both ways. As my friend Michael used to say, we need to think of worship in a spirit of generosity. My willingness to participate in a hymn or prayer that doesn't sit comfortably with me allows someone else to experience their favorite element of worship. And there lies the alternative to inclusive language: expansive language. Rather than trying to fit everything in, we need a generosity in our language that allows a whole variety of images and expressions. Rather than trying to whitewash it all to fit a narrow range of acceptability that doesn't leave anybody out or create any offense, we need to be bold enough to allow many specific expressions that come out of particular and diverse experiences and cultures.

Beyond Inclusive

In another one of our Advent Café sermon series, we studied the book of Acts. It's a powerful thing to journey with those first disciples in the remarkable, miraculous, astonishing spread of this community called the church. Any time that these people think that they have this new community figured out, and they understand their place in it and what they're doing, then things change.

Wendy was invited to preach on the night that we discussed Peter's dream telling him that all the off-limit foods of his Jewish faith were now considered clean, and the follow-up to that dream, which was the inclusion of Gentile (non-Jewish) people in the church circle too. But Wendy insightfully pointed out that much more than inclusion was happening. In bringing in the Gentiles,

Peter and the others were also going out. The walls that they thought were around their community were blown apart. What started as a deeply unsettling call to Peter and the others to step outside of their comfort zones led to a celebration of relationships they had never considered.

It is here, far beyond inclusion, that the church is most alive.

It's Just Beginning

Anita, the woman in our study who thought there might be room for "all of me" in our church, began a process of discernment several years after she came to St. George's. My priestly partner in crime, Scott, and I suspected that she was being called to be a deacon of the church, and that resonated with Anita as well. Anita leads our breakfast mentor program, a ministry of hospitality offered at St. George's daily breakfast. Anita understands how people get trapped: into using substances in order to survive; into an endless today, unable to see a future; into seeing themselves as alone, unable to access any offer of help around themselves. She ministers with humor, kindness, prayer, and great understanding to the people who come as guests to our breakfast program. When we first spoke to Anita about being a deacon, she reacted with joy and humility, and also with a caveat.

"I won't be preaching," she said. "That's not my gift."

As is so often the case, God didn't just call Anita outside the walls of our church to connect with those on the margins, God also called her outside of her own walls. Anita is brimming with theological insight, with a natural and powerful ability to connect our faith with the deepest needs of our hearts and of the heart of our world. A big part of Anita's journey has been finding her voice and using it.

She isn't waiting in the church for people to show up so she can tell them they can come in. Anita is out in the parking lot and in our breakfast room ministering to people in their pain right now, treating them as people of dignity and worth, caring for them, in whatever bad places they have gotten themselves into, as brothers and sisters. She knows each guest who comes to St. George's for breakfast; she knows the insight, the hard-earned wisdom, the pain and heartbreak and love that they bring to the table. Anita bears witness, to all of us, to the fuller picture of what it is to be church. The church is not contained or defined by buildings or membership lists or by even the most compelling invitations to join in with what we're doing. The church is most alive and most real in the interactions that reveal to us the God who is alive and real in all of us.

Perhaps that's the biggest downfall of calling ourselves an inclusive church. We think the work is finished here. And really, it's just beginning.

DISCUSSION QUESTIONS

1. The seeming good of being inclusive can be a foil for selfishness and self-righteousness. We want others to participate in the thing we love so that this thing can continue. We believe we have something others need; they are welcome to join us, if they become like us. Where do you see inclusivity as a good? Where is it problematic?

2. The church is the gathered community of faith. But why is the sending part of our community just as important as the gathering? What does the "sent" church look like?

3. Have you experienced this conflict around navigating change in the church when new people come in? What is good and life-giving about this?

4. When have you been challenged, blessed, and changed by the voice of someone who sees the world differently than you do?

CHAPTER 23

Embrace Our Prayer

After a few weeks of summer vacation, our church's leadership team met. Our agenda was a bulky one after the weeks of hiatus. First, we welcomed Carrie to our meeting. She had joined us ten months prior as our interim counselor in our Step Youth Resource Centre, and we wanted to offer her the full-time job as lead counselor.

We remarked on her commitment to the young people who came into Step for help, as well as her creativity and compassion in developing the programming to serve them. She shared that she had been homeless as a teenager. She had couch-surfed among friends for many years and had lived in the dangerous circumstances many of our Step clients also navigated. She talked about having good teachers who didn't give up on her and who insisted that she not be defined by her circumstances, but by the intelligence and compassion they saw in her. She did what she did because of what others saw in her.

Our meeting with Carrie was followed by a meeting with Ed, who is retired from the military and defines himself as a "professional pain in the ass." He is heavily involved in local politics, holding our municipal government to account on environmental issues, affordable housing, and living up to St. Catharines' self-appointed label as a "Compassionate City." He wanted to speak to our leadership about collaborating on an initiative to strengthen our city; he was interested in this collaboration because of our church's strong connection to the marginalized people of St. Catharines.

Unprompted, he shared a story very similar to Carrie's. He grew up in subsidized housing and in poverty. When we talked about "the marginalized," he recognized his lived reality. He told us about getting into trouble with the law as a kid and coming up before a judge for sentencing. The judge did not put him in jail, but said instead that he saw something in Ed and believed Ed could live a different sort of life, make better choices.

"Everything that I do now," he said, "is because of who I was then."

Of Course It's Connected

For about ten years, I was involved in what our church calls General Synod, the national meeting of representatives from across our country to make decisions and set a vision for our Anglican Church in Canada. It meets every three years.

Many important conversations happen at General Synod. That has been the primary forum for truth and reconciliation in our church with Indigenous people. For decades, the Indigenous and non-Indigenous church has been imagining what a self-determining Indigenous church would look like and how we might go forward together in partnership. It has been able to set the course for environmental action, for addressing human trafficking, and for taking steps (albeit slow ones) in decolonizing the Church.

Sometimes General Synod can be a hot mess. Particularly when we talk about sex and marriage, the message that we tell ourselves and that we put out to tell the world is a fraught and hurtful one.

What gets very little air time at General Synod is personal faith. What gets only minimally more air time is the prayer and worship of the Church. I have seen the Faith and Worship Committee of our national Church regularly get their agenda time sliced, diced, and shortened in favor of more debate on controversial topics.

I asked a question at the beginning of this book: "What if it's connected?" I was reflecting on that group of teens shooting up outside of our church building. I was reflecting on the suicide rates in Indigenous Canada. I was noting Archbishop Mark's insistence that what was happening in Indigenous Canada is a spiritual crisis. I was inviting us to see the aching needs of our world—the environmental degradation; the wildfires and floods;

the rising rates of depression, addiction, and suicide; the poverty in our streets and the desperation behind middle-class doors—as a spiritual crisis too. And I was asking whether it might be possible that my little story of crisis, of vocation, of heartbreak, of grace could be a response to this crisis. More importantly, I was asking whether *our* story could be a response to this crisis.

Carrie and Ed, both of them speaking not in religious language but reporting on their experience from the school and judicial systems, tell me that the answer to my question is a resounding yes. Our response is always born out of our story. Our offering is always formed out of what we have experienced. Of course it's connected.

Of course our social justice work, our advocacy, our commitment to social change, and our response to those who are hungry and in need in our community must be connected to our stories of grace, of transformation, of blessing, of how God has met us in the mess of our lives, of where we have been surprised by love, given second chances, and shown a way forward that we didn't know was possible. If we understand, as Archbishop Mark insists, that the hurt we see in the world around us is a manifestation of a spiritual crisis, a disconnection of our human lives from core spiritual truths, then yes, our personal stories can offer a point of reconnection. Our places of brokenness and of healing, of how we have fallen apart and how in falling apart we have received some measure of goodness and possibility and something new in us has been born, these are at the core of what drives any response that we might ever have to the hurt we encounter around us.

This response is not just for us, it's for everyone. Whatever we assume about the hurt of the world, we should assume that God is working there too. The story of how we are infected with one another and how God is at work is not a story for, or of, the church. It's everyone's story. As Carrie and Ed clearly show in their lives, those experiences of grace and love overflow to bless and serve others. Those stories of grace and love, shared, help us all to better attend to the truth of who we really are, what our lives are for.

Whatever the church looks like going forward, however the structure of the church necessarily must change and the institution must adapt, we have to intentionally connect in ourselves, and in our offering to the world, what has been connected all along. We have to insist that whatever we say or do in the world always starts here, in the ultrareal of God at work in our broken lives.

How Can Praise Be the Answer?

One night in late March of 2020, I met up with my friends Allison and Gerald on a Wednesday to livestream our regular worship service to an empty church because COVID-19 had sent us into lockdown. As they were setting up to lead the music that night, they told me of a difficult decision they were coming to that day. They are full-time touring musicians. They make their livelihood from their music ministry, Infinitely More. They relied on their two annual tours for about eight months of their annual income. Although they had still hoped for a truncated version of their East Coast tour, they were coming to the realization that they would have to cancel the whole thing.

"After Good Friday," they told me, "we don't have another for-sure event lined up until July." It was devastating on many levels. It wasn't just a question of finances, although that most certainly was consequential. "It's that we can't do what we love," Allison said. "This is what we're called to do, and we can't do it."

Before the first song, Allison noted for our online congregation that she and Gerald had selected the songs for the evening based on what they were hearing from people all across Canada who were connected to their music ministry. People wanted to be reminded of God's sovereignty when it felt like life is so out of control. They wanted to express their need for God's healing. But what they heard people expressing most of all was to be called back to a stance of praise. They needed to praise God. Allison and Gerald had just shared with me some of the most difficult circumstances that they have ever known professionally; moments later Allison was leading our people in the act of praising God.

On the surface, their response made no sense. It was sorrow more than anything that I was carrying into our worship that night. Allison and Gerald's situation seemed to embody all of the stories of anxiety, loss, illness, and fear that were piling up for each of us as COVID upended everything we thought we knew about normal life. Scott couldn't get through one service in the first months of the pandemic without choking up and visibly weeping, and that night was no different.

A weird thing happened as Allison and Gerald named the need for praise and then led us in offering it. The weird thing about the empty church livestream was that it didn't feel as weird as we thought it would. It felt like the great cloud of witnesses was viscerally real; it felt like the fellowship of the Holy Spirit was powerful. It felt like the loving presence of Jesus walked right beside us.

It did not feel like my questions were answered, the mysteries of the universe unlocked, or that Allison and Gerald were given a safe and secure income for the unsettled months ahead. But somehow we could all express the feeling of knowing we were loved and blessed. I was reminded that I have the capacity to express love too, and this reminder comes as a gift from on high. I felt small, and feeling small felt really honest. To praise God is to surrender all of my own limitations, to offer up my grief and worries, to choose to seek love and beauty simply because Love and Beauty have already sought me. It didn't make sense, and yet each of these surprising truths was viscerally real.

What If We Start Here?

The pandemic started for me that night. It started there because it was that moment that I needed to keep coming back to. It started there because it needed to start there, not just in the story of brokenness and God's promise and faithfulness in meeting us. It also started in our capacity to respond, to gather against all odds, to pray with one another even as the world was falling apart. To lift up our holy and broken "hallelujah." To praise God because it is in us to do so. It is in us to do so because of love.

Because we have been loved, we also in each and every moment can access our God-given capacity to love in return. That's what our praise is. It's our response of love. That's what Carrie and Ed were naming in that corporation meeting. They were naming their experience of being met with a surprising love and of devoting their lives to offering that love in return.

What is our response to the spiritual crisis in which we are living? It is ourselves. It is our voices lifted in prayer and song and great love. It is our stories of brokenness and blessing. It is the mess of who we are, and it's our hearts being shaped not just to receive the love of God but to give it too.

If I were to be given charge over our Church, if I were to list one area I most want to change, this would be it. It wouldn't start with waving a magic wand and decolonizing the Church, addressing the inequities that are still so much at work for our female leadership, having equal marriage accepted and Indigenous people's voices finally centered. I desperately want these changes for our Church, but I wouldn't start here. I also wouldn't start with filling our churches to the brim with young people and tithing families and all of the markers of success and fruitfulness.

I would start with making sure that our personal stories get lifted up in all of our decision-making, that our witness to the world isn't just how we want to fight for a more just future, but also how we have been met and transformed by God's grace. I would start by assuming that our prayer and praise is actually the most important thing that we have to offer because it is never just about ourselves, it is always about love, and most importantly, it is always about how our little lives can respond to God's love by loving back. It's about how everything we do has to be founded in that capacity to love in return.

I would start here and see what happens.

DISCUSSION QUESTIONS

1. Do you know of people like Ed and Carrie? People who, because of the difficulties and second chances they experienced, are now people of help and compassion for others?

2. How do you connect with the story of Allison and Gerald leading the church in praise as a response to life going off the rails? Why do you think praise is part of our life as a church? What does it mean to praise God?

3. Why might our stories of "being met by a surprising love" and "finding our capacity to love in return" be so important for the future of the church? How might our stories of "God meeting us in the mess" be central to who we are and how we go forward as a community of faith?

4. How can our stories of love and grace be a response to the world's need?

CHAPTER 24

Embrace the Story We Share

I've Been There Too

I decided to sign up for some ministry coaching at the end of 2020. I had worked with Peter Elliott on past projects for the national Church. I look up to him as someone who hasn't just led a church similar to St. George's in size and scope, but has also managed to keep a humble attitude and a good sense of humor and to compile a lot of practical and unpretentious wisdom along the way.

In our biweekly Zoom coaching sessions, we talked through a number of dilemmas, hopes, and dreams, identifying concrete next steps and longer-term strategies. What made the biggest difference to me were those moments when Peter was able to respond to one of my struggles with a story from his own experience. "I've been there too," became the solid ground in our coaching relationship, his offering to me that allowed me to breathe, to trust, to trust myself and my experience, because someone that I respect so much has been there too. In all of the other work that we looked at together, that starting point of companionship and understanding was an immeasurable treasure.

I started this book by saying that the problem that led me to the edge of ministry burnout wasn't the busyness of the job or the weight of responsibilities or that I had too much on my plate as a full-time working mom; it was that it didn't feel like anything was working anymore.

"This wasn't in the fine print," was a refrain in my sessions with Peter. I became a priest in order to care for people. Instead, I found myself dealing every day with the nuts and bolts of running a budget, a staff, all of the legal and human resource bits and pieces that go along with a million-dollar-a-year ministry enterprise.

"Yes, it's a church," a number of my friends said sympathetically. "But it's also a business."

Running a business is not what I signed up for. And the constant unhappiness I was encountering every day across the parish seemed to add weight to the suspicion that I was not cut out for this. The "I've been there too" that Peter offered helped to reframe my feelings and my experience. He told me of his own similar experiences and frustrations. He normalized the disconnect I had been feeling ministering so far outside of the bounds of our usual human interactions during COVID. Because of the sharing of his experience, I began to see something in my own.

Yes, there is a business element to this religious institution, and also it's a church. What I mean by that is that the church isn't some separate idealized entity. It's full of politics. It requires money. And it is made up of messy, complicated, sometimes infuriating, and difficult people. If I go back to my priestly job description—to lift up—the truth is that all of it gets lifted up, not just the nice and ethereal and healed and whole parts. The ins and outs of the institution, the human resource dramas, the budget worries, the complaints and disappointments and the not-enough of all of our lives, it all gets lifted up. And when I, as a parish leader, am attending to the more business elements of how it all comes together, I am also practicing my priestly ministry because the truth is that it's all part and parcel of the same human reality.

That's where God promises to meet us. Not in some scrubbed-clean and untainted reality of the church, but in this muddle that includes finances and legal concerns and some really crappy decisions that sometimes have to be made. Those really crappy decisions aren't made outside of my responsibilities as a priest and my love for God's people, but as part of the bargain, the work that I'm called to, and the promise that in all of the fracture and mistakes and shortcomings that are of course our reality, God will meet us there with healing and new life. And love.

You May Think I'm Crazy, but . . .

Cheryl and Sarah and I were having lunch. Cheryl and Sarah are both visible and respected leaders in our Anglican Church. When they speak, people listen. They each have had an experience of God's healing hand at a critical juncture in their lives. As I mentioned earlier in this book, Cheryl was hit by a car when she was a child and airlifted to a hospital, where her parents were told she would either die or remain in a permanent vegetative state. When she woke up from her coma, she told her astonished family that she had seen a deceased uncle who had sent her back to them. Many years later, she ran into the surgeon who looked after her case, who admitted that her recovery was one of those inexplicable miracles in his medical experience.

Sarah shared her own story in response to Cheryl's. She has suffered throughout her life with ulcerative colitis and got to a point where none of the treatments were working. Her strength and her body were visibly failing, and Sarah was hospitalized. As family and medical professionals were wringing their hands in desperation, she heard a voice tell her that she would be all right. Sarah had turned away from her faith in anger over how much suffering her illness was causing her, but in that moment she felt drawn back. Her anger dissipated. Her family were stunned and a little frightened by the sudden peacefulness of her demeanor. She began to recover shortly thereafter and reoriented her life toward Christian service.

Both women couched their spiritual experiences in a similar way. "I know there are other explanations for this," or "you might not believe this," or even that all-too-easy catchphrase, "you may think I'm crazy but . . ." They had profound, life-saving experiences of spiritual realities affecting their actual physical well-being, and they wanted to make sure in telling their stories that we realized that they knew how improbable all of it was.

Cheryl called them both out. "Isn't it interesting how even as people of faith, talking to other people of faith, we have to tell our story in this way? We know that something happened to us, but we want to make sure that nobody thinks that we actually fully believe it happened to us. Even as people of faith, we feel a need to explain it away."

As she spoke, I was flooded with memories. I am a priest of the church, and yet how many times have I had quiet conversations with faithful parishioners preempted by their whispered words, "You may think I'm crazy, but . . ."

Such is the typical framework for the mainline church's testimony. "You may think I'm crazy, but . . ." Quiet, whispered, intimate, and private conversations, experiences told with apology or even fear because these are the kinds of things that people like us just don't openly talk about. For the mystics in our midst, for the ones for whom the experience of God's guiding voice and loving presence is just so real and visceral that doubt doesn't even factor in, for them the fear can be paralyzing.

"I dream dreams," a fellow colleague in ministry told me on break from a national Church meeting. This is a woman whose expertise and wisdom is admired and respected all across our Church. "God speaks to me in dreams. But I would never share that around this table."

"I hear God's voice all the time," a choir member told me in a whisper at coffee hour one morning. "I am really careful about who I share that with."

Cheryl was right; there is something strange about a bunch of religious people being afraid to talk about our experiences of God. She also named a growing edge for our particular way of being church. We can get better at sharing our stories because doing so helps others to share their stories too. When we become more comfortable with talking about our faith, that can also have a positive impact on how we then live that faith out.

At the same time, there is something exceptional and compelling about the framework of "you may think I'm crazy, but . . ." When I was chatting with my friend Kate about this, she had an interesting observation, which is that "you may think I'm crazy" is a sort of testimony we can take seriously. It is testimony that eschews "clubiness" and insider cliché. It makes room. It makes room for people, both part of our churches and not part of our churches, to consider joining us in naming experiences that don't fit into our reasonable expectations and our everyday language. We can keep our feet firmly planted in the realm of all that we think we logically and reasonably know. And we can also wonder together at those glimmers of uncommon sense that shimmer across our lives. We can be part of how those glimmers become easier to see the more we train our eyes to look at what is really going on.

However we choose to share, whether it's quietly, with caveats, or with unguarded enthusiasm for what has happened, there is something important about these stories that allows others to consider their own stories too. There is a permission offered for others to hear that maybe "I've been there too."

We Believe

Most of our worship services invite us at some point to stand up and recite together one of the church's creeds. In a middle-of-the-road Anglican service, that will be either the Apostles' Creed or the Nicene Creed. Both offer a three-part affirmation of our faith in God the Father, God the Son, and God the Holy Spirit. Various other statements of faith have been developed or pulled from scripture in order to offer that same opportunity to affirm our Christian faith together but with words that feel fresher.

I find this moment to be one of the most awkward things about our worship service. No matter how beautiful the music, how poignant the sermon, how spiritual the flow of everything else, this moment in basically the dead center of our worship is when—no matter who you are, whether you are new to Christianity or a longtime Christian, whether you are visiting for a baptism or just beginning to wonder about faith, or whether you are totally convicted by all of it—we are all expected to express a unity of belief that almost certainly isn't there.

Various solutions to this awkwardness have been tried. For a while, it was fashionable for liberal Christians to remain silent for the parts of the creed that they didn't believe. In our church, we like to introduce the creed with some words of context and permission: "Recognizing that we are all at different points on our faith journey, if you are able to join in the creed, our Christian statement of hope, then please do so."

I have often wondered whether the creeds have relevancy for today's congregations. How much are people really thinking about what they're saying? How important is it for people to subscribe to each of the tenets we proclaim in order to count themselves as part of our church? Certainly in our tradition, the unity of the Church does not come from being confessional. As my friend and colleague Michael has coined it, "You don't have to believe to belong." We belong by virtue of being gathered at God's table and fed by God's hand of love, not because we have all signed on the dotted line confirming that we subscribe to the same tenets of faith. And yet, the longer that I serve in ministry, the more value I experience in the faith we share together. While we might individually struggle with particular beliefs, or for that matter struggle to be able to lift our voices in prayer and hope to God at all, the boat that we're in together promises us a way through the choppy seas.

Alan McLean is a member of our congregation, a retired United Church minister, and a constant voice of wisdom and insight in our community's conversations. He speaks about praying the psalms in his individual prayer life. There are many parts of the psalms that represent emotions and experiences to which he himself doesn't connect. But he prays those parts anyway, because he knows that his voice is helping to uphold others in prayer in their very different circumstances and emotional landscapes. He actively remembers that there is actually no such thing as praying alone. We're always tapping into the "great cloud of witnesses," both alive and passed, who are praying with us too.

Alan has helped me love the creeds again because it gives the community a powerful opportunity to support one another in faith. I personally don't have to believe everything that we say together. I can allow this community of prayer and spiritual experience to believe for me in the parts and the moments when I myself find it hard to believe. That flies directly in the face of our most basic individualistic assumptions, but it is incredibly liberating. It's okay if I don't believe right now because I'm part of this community that holds the faith collectively, holds me in my disbelief, and points to something much bigger than just my own narrow field of vision.

Ad Hoc Water Stations and a Homemade Finish Line

My road back from burnout recovery included a homemade finish line at the end of a virtual marathon. I was at a low point when Brian insisted that I gather that circle of friends together for support and admit to them that I wasn't really coping. That, in and of itself, helped. That small group, along with my husband, kids, and some other dear friends, provided a foundation of trust and friendship that allowed me to admit that I wasn't doing very well.

Around the same time, I began meeting with Peter in a mentoring relationship. "I've been there too" became a soft place to land when the decisions that I was having to make in ministry on a daily basis felt too impossibly hard.

Our church can give us a flood of popular Jesus images, along with hymns and prayers that sing to our triumphant, radiant, death-defying Jesus. What can get lost in all of this triumph is the very different kind of power Jesus accessed throughout his ministry. In the wilderness, in the quiet moments of prayer, in the Garden of Gethsemane and on the cross, we see that the offering of Jesus's ministry is grounded in his own weakness and vulnerability. He leads by going into every dark and fragile corner of what it means to be human, what it means to be haunted by demons, to need the tender care of another, to have his heart broken, to experience his own body failing, and to expel his final breath. He teaches his followers not how to be strong, but how to be totally and completely human. He teaches them to hunger, to need healing, to ask forgiveness, to give thanks, to not know everything, to be surprised, and to take up the cross as the walking wounded and follow Jesus on the pathway of love.

In the new year of 2021, I began training for a marathon. Although I had been running for about fifteen years, I had never even once considered making a marathon a goal. I had actively ruled out ever doing so. Whenever I came to the finish line of a half-marathon, I knew without a doubt that I would never ever be able, or want, to run another 21.1 kilometers on top of what I had already run to complete a half. That was a feat too extraordinary to even contemplate.

But 2021 dawned with the second wave of COVID wreaking havoc on all of our lives. The first half of 2021 was mostly spent under stay-at-home orders in the province of Ontario.

We were allowed to go out for exercise, though. Running has, throughout my time as a priest, been a mainstay of my spiritual well-being, not to mention my physical and emotional well-being too. It's where I feed my inner introvert; it's how I step back from situations in order to reflect rather than just react; it's my stockpile of endorphins that provide a mood passport through situations that would otherwise emotionally sink me.

So I made a plan to run.

Although I run alone, and although I love running alone, I don't really ever run by myself. Julie, Janice, Janine, Dianne, Kent, and Jeff are my go-to running friends who helped me with training, stretching, and nutrition plans for the months ahead. They checked in with me throughout to encourage and motivate and advise. My nonrunning friends did too. My marathon goal became a goal that my circle of friends and family invested in with me.

I signed up for the virtual Saskatchewan Marathon. In 2020 and 2021, most races that were held were virtual ones, which meant you ran your race where you were, used a running watch or app to track your time and distance, and posted your results afterwards. This virtual race allowed me to join a race taking place in Saskatoon from my neck of the woods in Niagara, three thousand kilometers away. At the end of May, my race bib, T-shirt, and finisher's medal arrived in the mail. June 19 was race day.

To say the training was intense is an obvious statement. About two-thirds of the way through, when all I seemed to be doing was running and recovering from running, it felt impossible. On Jeff's advice, I planned out five thirty-plus-kilometer runs over the course of training in order to prepare for the final distance of 42.2 kilometers. On my thirty-four-kilometer distance run, my mind went to some dark and fretful places. I clocked the seventeen-kilometer mark, and realizing I was only halfway through, nearly gave up. When I finally stumbled home at the end, I agonized about how I could possibly add on another eight kilometers beyond that to attain the required distance on race day.

It was around this time that a number of people started reaching out to me to ask if they could help on the day of the marathon. Julie and Janine and Britt offered to run part of the way with me. Tom and his daughter, my goddaughter Ivy, wanted to have music playing at the finish line. John and Ann and Beth realized that I would need water stations along the way, and Ann took it upon herself to organize and staff these for me. Paul and Sue were at every water station, from 5:30 a.m. onward, and in between water stations, they circled by my route in order to cheer me on along the way.

June 19 was a hot, humid day. All week, the forecast had promised rain, and instead, the sun came out after an overnight thunderstorm, creating circumstances that felt a lot like a steam bath. I had planned my sports drink and my fueling needs very carefully based on my training, but my plan fell short for the actual conditions of the day. When I got to the last water station, with seven kilometers left to go, I realized that I didn't have enough fluid to address my wild, sweaty thirst. Paul grabbed an extra water bottle from his car and gave me that to top myself up.

Brian had come to the last station on his bike, feeling that it might be a good idea if he cycled behind me for the last leg. When he had suggested it the day before, it had sounded unnecessary to me, but like I have said before, Brian's ideas are usually good ones, so I said yes. Again I ran out of water on that last stretch, and this time it was Brian to save the day, refilling my water bottle from his own. He also passed over to me a few energy chews, which gave me the added boost I needed to keep going and to knock out the last few kilometers. When I was rounding the corner into my neighborhood and the promised finish line, Brian cycled ahead to tell everyone I was on my way. About twenty masked friends and family cheered me across a ribbon finish line held by my mom and the kids. Ivy had "The Girl Is On Fire" pumping over a little karaoke machine. John placed a laurel wreath on my head. Gordon went to fetch me a big icy-cold glass of restorative chocolate milk.

I know how privileged I am to have people show up for me like that. I know the blessing of being able-bodied and training for a marathon as a way of attending to my emotional and spiritual health. These are specific and incredible blessings.

That marathon finish line is exactly an image of the church—who we are, why we continue to show up for one another, what it's all about. We are people who don't run alone, who actually can't run alone. We are people who can fill in the gaps for one another, who must fill in the gaps for one another. We are people who are charged with figuring out a makeshift finish line and homemade water stations when all of the rest of the world has been overturned. We are people whose small bits of belief, insight, dedication, and training don't add up to a whole lot on our own, but together we can get somewhere. That somewhere attests to a truth and a power that is greater than us, greater than the sum of our parts, that embodies life and death and resurrection and hope and healing and need and the beauty of the finish line and all of the water stations along the way.

When we say "we believe" together in our church services, we aren't being straitjacketed into a one-size-fits-all faith. Our statements of faith are general enough to leave a lot of room for our varied experiences, as well as our honest and searching doubts. What we are doing is embracing one another, choosing one another. This embrace can look a lot like cobbling together some water stations along the marathon of life. We don't just have to be stuck with one another; we can show up for each other. And we can admit that we can't do this alone and that there is a truth and power that is far bigger than the sum of our parts. "No matter what happens," the late author Brian Doyle famously wrote, "this happened."

No matter what happens, there is the truth of how the healing power of God was made known in a circle of people who happened, through the gift of the church, to be part of my life.

I wouldn't have crossed the finish line without them.

DISCUSSION QUESTIONS

1. What is your experience of having creeds, or statements of faith, in worship? Do you find it awkward, like Martha, or is it meaningful to you?

2. Why is the sharing of experience, the "I've been there too," so powerful? Are there times when that is not a helpful way of responding to one another?

3. Martha notes that the church doesn't exist as a rarified and separate reality, but involves politics, finances, crummy decisions, and difficult people? Why is this important to remember?

4. Do you find that people in your faith community share their stories of how and where they have experienced God at work? Do those stories come easily? Do they get framed in that way of "you may think I'm crazy . . ."? What is important or life-giving about the sharing of these stories?

5. Where do you experience the church embracing its ability to show up for one another? How do you connect to the image of the cobbled-together finish line and the makeshift water stations of Martha's marathon run? How is this an image for the church?

CHAPTER 25

Embrace Apocalypse

Pulling Back the Curtain

In 2021, Simone Biles was the far-and-away favorite to pick up all the available gymnastic medals at the Summer Olympics. Commentators were already anointing her as the greatest gymnast of all time, tallying up what the coming medals would mean for the many Olympic records she was about to break. Instead, Biles pulled out of the competition and cheered her teammates from the sidelines. She was not obviously injured, and so the conclusion—which she in short order confirmed—was that the injury that she had suffered must be a mental one.

"It's not that athletes haven't been suffering before," one astute broadcaster noted. "But what Simone Biles is doing in this moment is pulling back the curtain so that we can see." She is such a formidable competitor and respected titan of the sport that her withdrawal had to be taken seriously as a pain and an injury that is as real as a snapped tendon, even if it doesn't show up on an X-ray in the same way.

That language of "pulling back the curtain" made me wonder if that broadcaster might be a Christian.

The word apocalypse doesn't refer to the end of the world. It is from the Greek verb apocalypto, and it means "to unveil" or "to reveal." It is a pulling back of the curtain on current times to describe the spiritual truth of what is happening. Media theorist Marshall McLuhan was once asked whether he was optimistic or pessimistic about the future. Based on the conviction of his Christian faith, he responded, "I am not an optimist or a pessimist. I'm an apocalyptic." Christians consider apocalyptic thought as fundamentally hopeful. It is a stripping away of the lies we tell ourselves, a revealing of what is true. It is the affirmation that we have the God-given capacity to turn our lives away from the lies and back toward that truth. It's not that mental suffering wasn't always happening in the realm of top-tier athletes, but it took a brave young woman to pull back the curtain in order to show us.

The Ultrareal of the Church Gathered

Dan and I were able to plan a spontaneous trip to Rome one October, just months before COVID-19 shut down the world. We made few concrete plans other than to make the trek to St. Paul-Outside-the-Walls, the site of the martyrdom and burial of the apostle Paul. We had been to Rome several times, but the draw to the city's center is strong, and we hadn't made it out to this site before.

I wanted to honor Paul's role in my life. At the age of fifteen, I had read the Bible for the first time. I was smitten with Jesus, with his wit and his ability to see the world in ways that I had never considered. But when I met Paul in the Acts of the Apostles and in his writings, I knew that I was home. Here was a chronic overachiever just like me. And here was the articulation of grace—my anxious striving to measure up leveled by a love that I couldn't (and didn't need to) earn.

There were public transit options, but we wanted to approach as pilgrims, so we walked. St. Paul-Outside-the-Walls is well named. You get there by walking right out of the crowds of the bustling city, past its ancient walls, and onto streets where ordinary people live and work. The tourists thin out and then disappear all together. It was a welcome change. It was even more welcome when we finally approached the massive basilica and, as opposed to every other place we had gone in Rome, all we could see was empty space. There were a few buses lined up to drop off visitors, but their numbers were insignificant in the face of the site's epic dimensions and cavernous silence.

My relief at being out of the crush of loud, gawking, jostling, self-absorbed tourists was short lived. My awe at the dimensions and majesty of the basilica turned into a growing disquiet. Hung around the sanctuary were two sets of pictures: the top set pictured every pope of Rome, from Peter to Francis I; the bottom set depicted thirty-six key moments in the life of Paul. Not surprisingly, the top set of pictures were all of white men, most of them bearded. But the weight of this visual was amplified by the way that Paul's life was also depicted. In the thirty-six images, only one had a woman in it—a small girl being freed from demon possession. As I looked around at the statuary and art contained in the basilica, these two sets of images left me only able to see what wasn't there. The story of the church had been scrubbed clean of the ethnically diverse and egalitarian community of faith that Paul was so much a part of midwifing into existence across Rome. The witness of the misfits—of women and slaves raised as leaders in this mushrooming community and the comingling of people across tribe and race, all because of the radical hospitality of God—was exchanged for a picture of the church that has opted instead to cozy up to the values of the empire.

Back in the city's center, this cozy relationship was also prominently visible. There is no denying that the church has long shared the values of the patriarchy. Across the Christian church— even the parts of the church where women have been ordained for a generation or two—that has been hard to alter. But it was in being outside the walls of Rome that day that allowed me to see clearly why I love the city inside those walls so much. I love Rome because, unwittingly and often unwillingly, this is a city who can't help but sing the song of Mary.

In scripture, we meet Mary as a young, brave girl who was asked to do an impossible thing: to become pregnant with Jesus outside of the safe confines of marriage. Accolades and titles, crowns and thrones of heaven have been assigned to her for her courage in saying yes to God's plan. But when she was first pregnant and unwed, she was just a girl in trouble running to the safe haven of her relative Elizabeth. Elizabeth's inner eye went into overdrive when Mary walked through the door, and Elizabeth was able to confirm for Mary that the God of all, the Creator of the universe, was in fact at work in this irregular pregnancy— words that must have inspired both relief and terror in Mary.

In response to this relief and terror, Mary did a strange thing. She sang. She sang words of praise and upset. She sang of God's power, loose and unsettling in her own life, and she sang of God's power dismantling even the most staid institutions, humbling the most secure and admired and authoritarian people among us. She sang of truth, how God is actually at work, whether we like it or not: "The mighty will be cast from their thrones, and the little ones will be lifted up." Mary sang of love. As her own life seemed to be falling apart, her future compromised, she nonetheless responded to the inconvenient and disruptive and terrifying power of God with words of gratitude and love.

In Rome, there is this complicated relationship with empire, but that brave, prophetic, and wise female voice is the sweet and strong descant that refuses to be silenced, that lilts untouchable and unstoppable above the competing voices. Yes, there are plaques of popes and legions of collared men roaming the streets. But alongside this dominant story of white male leadership is the actual living reality of the church gathered. Beyond any church programs, beyond worries of decline and plans for growth, beyond religious weaponization and the use of the church to prop up the agendas of the mighty, there is this ultrareal of the church. This is who we really are, and this truth of who we really are always and eventually comes out.

Historical saints like Agnes and Cecilia, women of self-possession, are lifted up alongside the fishermen and no-account peasants. In St. Bartholomew's, a beautiful church on an island in the Tiber River, the lay-led Sant'Egidio's community has collected and displayed relics telling the story of sainthood still being lived out across the world—by all genders, all races, numerous denominations, different levels of education and influence, young and old. Every one of these witnesses, from Jesus through to the faithful today struggling against the oppressive and dehumanizing power of empire, looked as if they were powerless in the face of the Caesars and Hitlers of history. But it is their feeble artifacts that ultimately have been lifted up and venerated with the lingering, growing power to instill faith in our hearts.

Outside the relentless crush of Roman tourists, I realized how much I missed the crowd. There aren't enough traffic lights, bathrooms, or sidewalks to accommodate Rome's volume of visitors, and nobody obeys the rules about silence and no pictures in the holiest of sites. Yet these jostling masses are also the counterpoint to the church's propensity for whitewashing our story. The male leaders of the church are here, and they are front and center. But those crowds tell a story too.

This is the church that is faithless; this is the church that wants to be faithful and can turn around at any point and hear again that leveling call of mercy and grace. This is the church of tourists with jaws on the floor gawping at every sparkling attraction; this is the church on its knees, still able to see holiness in the witness of insignificant, no-account people doing foolish things, like standing up to machine guns and giving to the poor. This is the rainbow church flaming so brightly it is hidden in plain sight; this is the church that doth protest too much. This is the church debating about whose marriage is valid and still not sure about the place of women—and yet, we are already here and we are leaders. The church is us too.

We descend on the city by the thousands—millions, even— all of us visibly searching for something. That is what Paul was so good at; the flame he fanned across the Roman Empire was the same one sparked by Jesus: connecting that hunger inside us with the one who has forever been seeking us.

The Funny Thing . . .

I have beaten my head against the wall at the frustrations of the institutional church, the ways in which I have been hampered and underestimated as a woman, the disappointments of ideas not being recognized and hurts being leveled and the institution being consistently stuck in thought patterns and assumptions and ways of being that work to preserve its own institutional life and lose sight of the renewing resurrection power of God. I have watched friends of mine in ministry get steamrolled by the institutional cruelty of the church. I have heard the institution debate the validity of people's marriage in ways that are demoralizing and traumatizing. I have been horrified by the uncovering of our systemic racism and the realization of how much we have aligned ourselves with the agenda of colonization.

And I have witnessed the God who is at work in us anyway.

Several days after our trip to St. Paul's, Dan and I found ourselves at the closing papal mass for the Synod on the Amazon. It had been taking place during our visit. In its final report, and from the papal chair in Pope Francis's closing homily, declarations were made about stewardship for the environment, a humble relationship of mutual learning with Indigenous people and the door cracked open for recognizing different forms of leadership—including married men in remote parts of the church, as well as female deacons. On both sides of the conservative–liberal divide, the declarations were greeted with anger and consternation. On one end was the accusation that Christ was being abandoned for paganism. On the other end, the church was criticized for once again falling so far short of aligning itself with the radical roots of a Savior whose mother evidently taught him about how the power of God really moves.

The funny thing about this synod is the funny thing about all of our church meetings, our plans and debates, the way that we try to organize and codify how we will or won't recognize the power of God on the move in us and in the world. The funny thing is that it's already happening, and God isn't looking for our permission. The funny thing is that the church is led by and alive in the brokenhearted, the little ones, and the overlooked, and it would be nice, but it's not necessary, for our church policies to get on board with this. The funny thing is that we are the church. We don't get to pick who is part of us or how God is going to be at work in us. But our hearts might be a lot better tuned in to the love of God if we just assumed that it's going to be in the mess, the brokenness, the infection of how our lives get mixed up and messed up with one another, where God will be powerfully at work.

Rome is an inspiring city and a hilarious city. It is hilarious and also profoundly tragic to see our two-thousand-year history, layered like a lasagna right in front of us, with the jostling crowds bearing witness to the truth each in their own little way, and to see in that history a truth that is happening right in front of our nose and that so easily escapes us. It is Cecilia and Agnes, it is the fishermen and the slaves, the female leaders and the gay leaders and the nonbinary leaders, leaders of every different color and background, in whom God has been powerful and at work all along. Like it or not, we are the church.

And it is in us that God acts.

Growing Churches . . .

When I was at St. David in Orillia, we were part of a study by Dr. David Haskell looking at trends in growing churches. Members of the staff and the congregation had to fill out extensive surveys, and Dr. Haskell did a site visit to our congregation. Some of his findings were eventually published, and a synopsis of his work was shared with all of the churches that participated. The takeaway from his work was boiled down to a rather oversimplified suggestion that churches that embrace more traditional teachings have a better chance of growing.[1] But when I spoke to him on the phone shortly after he completed his work, he offered me a much more compelling, and I would say insightful, bottom line.

"Growing churches expect God to act," he said.

That resonates because it gets beyond a bunch of superficial markers of what is and isn't successful in reaching out to people, and it takes us back to the most important question of all: Who are we? If we know who we are, then we also know why we do this, why we think that being the church matters.

This is not a book offering a manual on how to save the institutional church by bolstering numbers, attracting Gen Z and millennials, growing income and attendance all the while. It's a book inviting us to see with fresh eyes who we really are as Christians and as the church. It's a book inviting us to lean into that identity

---

1   An October 26, 2021, *New York Times* article, "Why 'Evangelical' Is Becoming Another Word for 'Republican'" by Ryan Burge (https://www.nytimes.com/2021/10/26/opinion/evangelical-republican.html) argues that the so-called staying power of evangelical Christianity against the forces of secularism has little to do with the effectiveness of their Christian teaching and more to do with evangelical Christianity becoming aligned with conservative politics.

and to choose it again. We aren't just stuck with one another. We embrace one another.

What Haskell was really saying in this quiet conversation about his research is in fact a one-sentence summary of the underlying "real" of the stories that have peppered this book. Who are we? Who is the church?

I think of Sarah and Cheryl. I think of Janine and James, Caitlyn and Ed and Carrie, Lorenzo and Tanya, Kevin and Danah, Linda and Alan and Aidan and Anita and so many others. I think of Archdeacon Val Kerr and Archbishop Mark MacDonald and the strong Indigenous leaders of our church, who haven't given up on this thing called church quite simply because they know who the church is and they can't help but keep calling us back to that. I think of Kelly Brown Douglas, Stephanie Spellers, and Winnie Varghese calling out the whiteness of the institutional church, even as they lead and serve our Church in ways that participate in the reforming and renewing power of God.

This is the church. For better and for worse, we've been gathered up in this thing together, and together we have seen how God has acted. Whatever we know or don't know, we know that we don't do this alone. We're not our musical choices or our packaging. We're a people drawn into relationship with the God who is at work in us and in our world.

And we look with expectation for how God is powerful and reaching out to us across all of our human brokenness.

I suspect the reason why churches who name the presence and activity of God at work in them, and in the world, tend to grow is because that language and those stories give others, not in our churches, permission and language to name the truth of how God is at work in them too. Because what we must assume is that God's activity most certainly isn't confined to us.

Our job is to keep gathering so that we can stay close to that truth, so that we can get better at seeing what God is up to, so that we can be tuned into the curtain getting pulled back and the mystery of God's powerful love being revealed to us and in us.

We keep gathering in witness to that point of connection that is true for all of us, not just the religious people: that we are stuck with each other, and we can choose one another, and the God of grace and love is even now drawing near in us. We keep gathering because this witness to connection and truth is a life-giving offering for the brokenness of our world.

This Is the Church

I spent about six months making weekly trips to SickKids hospital in Toronto to be with a family whose two-year-old son was dying in front of them as he waited for a heart transplant. SickKids is one of the leading pediatric hospitals in the world. My father, accompanying me on one of my trips to see Grayson, noted as he sat in the lobby that everyone is there, everyone at that hospital. There are people who have money. There are people who are barely scraping by. There are people speaking one of Canada's official languages, and those speaking tongues we would describe as foreign. There are people bearing the signs and symbols of their particular race, religion, and cultural background. There are those who blend into our conception of the dominant culture. Each of these people are receiving the best medical care for their children, not because they can afford it, not because they are the right kind of people or know the right kind of people, but because their children need it.

What I discovered at SickKids is that the hospital doesn't just run on a radical commitment to equality and cutting-edge medical expertise. It also runs on prayer. It was like the whole hospital was draped in this curtain of basic secular assumptions, and if you just tugged a little bit on that curtain, it fell back and you could see that the underside of this vast, state-of-the-art medical operation was running on prayer, on a powerful attentiveness to the nearness of God's love. If given the opportunity to do so, staff would talk about their own prayer lives that allowed them to slip needles painlessly into tiny little veins, that gave them strength to journey with families through their many stories of death and resurrection, that gave them eyes to see and nurture joy and hope and healing and possibility in the most desperate and difficult of circumstances.

This is the church. This is a vision not of who the church might be or could be or should be. This is the church that is. This is the church of the jostling crowds of Rome, the hallways of Sick-Kids, the parking lot of St. George's, and the strong song of Mary, singing of our demise and of the resurrection power of God. This is the church because this is where God is powerfully at work in our lives and in our world, whether we see it or not, name it or not, wrap it up in a nice religious bow or not.

This is the church who has been thrown together, cobbled together, gathered together. This is the church looking around and seeing that we're stuck with one another. This is the church figuring out the joy of getting to choose one another after all.

It is here, in that choice and that embrace, that the hope and promise and ultrareal of the church is found. It is here that we lift up a truth of connection and binding, infection and blessing, that is essential and life-giving for our whole aching, searching, lonely world. It is here that, together, we keep nudging that curtain back to tell the story of God's love drawn near.

DISCUSSION QUESTIONS

1. "Growing churches expect God to act." This isn't a book about church growth, but what do you find hopeful, or challenging, about this statement? Why might church growth be connected to this faithful expectation?

2. "We don't get to pick who is part of us or how God is going to be at work in us. But our hearts might be a lot better tuned in to the love of God if we just assumed that it's going to be in the mess, the brokenness, the infection of how our lives get mixed up and messed up with one another, where God will be powerfully at work." How is this a helpful reminder of what it is to be the church? How do you experience the truth of this statement?

3. The church is powerful and life-giving as it "nudges the curtain" to become more attentive to God's power and presence at work in our lives. How can the church be better at nudging the curtain to tell this story? Why is this important?

Acknowledgments

This book got started during my 2018 sabbatical leave. Thank you to the Kerley family, Jen Lang, and Catherine Pate for hosting me at their homes during that time and giving me space and inspiration to begin imagining my next book project.

Why Gather? started in one place and ended up in another. Thank you to the many faithful and patient readers along the way for the input, conversations, insight, and wisdom in shaping these ideas: Kate Crane, Matthew Townsend, Amanda Towe, David Harrison, Tom Vaughan, Dawn Davis, Kevin Block, Max Woollaver, Christyn Perkons, and Louise Peters. Thank you to Sarah Kingstone, who was offering me the gift of coaching in Energy Management when this book was beginning to coalesce, and who provided a wise sounding board for fine-tuning ideas. And thank you to my amazing editor, Milton Brasher-Cunningham, for believing in this project from the start while also being willing to keep sending me back to the drawing board in order to allow ideas to percolate and develop into the fuller potential he never gave up on seeing. I am glad and grateful for the whole Church Publishing family for their faith in their authors and their devotion to the work of expanding and growing meaningful conversations between our Church and our world about why the things we do and believe matter.

Thank you to Allison Lynn, who is not only always up for dessert, but is also full to overflowing with amazing ideas for how to navigate and grow in creative and artistic pursuits. And thank you to Linda Telega, who has made it clear that she knows how to throw the most glorious parties and is always willing to plan the best possible book launch celebration for this or any future book.

Thank you to St. George's, St. Catharines, and St. David, Orillia, whose people's faith forms the backbone of this book. I am blessed beyond measure in getting to serve with these brave, generous, and faith-filled communities of people. Thank you for sharing your stories with me, as well as permitting me to share your stories with this audience.

Thank you to the many dear friends from the various parts and places of my journey, both inside and outside of the church, who have my back no matter what. I hope you know who you are and what you mean to me.

Thank you to my family, my mom and dad, Susan and John; my brother, Andrew, and sister-in-law Jessica; my husband's sister, Julie; and my niece and nephew, Van and Jordan. You provide the steadiest foundation of love and support, which allows me to pursue all sorts of ventures, including writing this book.

Thank you to my husband, Dan, and my children, Cecilia and Gordon. The initial spark for this book came from some wise and wide-ranging conversations Gordon and I had on our many long walks (and sometimes when bedtime was being avoided). Those ideas then got to form more completely during a number of COVID lockdowns and stay-at-home orders. We not only didn't kill each other during all of that time stuck at home, we will no doubt look back on that time with each other, along with our two funny dogs, as some of our best and favorite memories. Thank you to each of you for blessing me with your insight and making our home into a place where we can laugh, discern, explore, wonder, hope, and open our hearts in love.

Lightning Source UK Ltd.
Milton Keynes UK
UKHW020713160622
404513UK00007B/422